Authors: Dina Manzo, Cho Phillips.
Technical Writer: Lynette Archer.
Book Design: Frank Muniz.
Photographers: Frederic Choisel, Adrian Soto, Michael Jensen.
Production Assistance: MB Weddings.
Guest: Linda Lehmann.

Location: Palazzo Della Montagna.
Supplies: Angie Zimmerman Designs, Napa Valley Linens, Classic Party Rentals, Mimi & Co.
Chef: Randall Selland from The Selland's Group.
Stylist: Elizabeth Galinda.
Makeup & Hair: Elle Couch, Camille Goldston.

Welcome to Dina Manzo's
"It's My Party and I'll Plan if I Want to"

This course was inspired to empower the desire to celebrate life's milestones while creating memories to last a lifetime with family and friends.

The creative passion for entertaining those we love and care about is in all of us, but many lack the information on how to begin, plan, and execute a social gathering without the stress of it all. This course is the answer to entertaining with ease and peace of mind. Knowing you have covered all your bases and being certain your guests experience will unfold exactly as you have envisioned provides confidence to any host.

We hope you enjoy Dina Manzo's Party Planning Series of courses:

- Dinner Party
- Bridal Shower
- Birthday
- Graduation
- Engagement
- Anniversary
- Quinceañera
- Retirement
- Wedding
- Baby Shower
- Holiday
- Family Reunions

For additional course information visit us at www.Lovegevity.com.

Lovegevity

© 2014 - Copyright by Lovegevity, Inc. All Rights Reserved.

Lovegevity's mission is to empower entrepreneurs to pursue their passion through education and provide a career path leading to a successful balance of life, career, and family.

Table of Contents

Introduction

- 10. Why Do We Entertain?
- 10. Course Outline
- 11. Course Navigation
- 12. Course Goals & Objectives
- 13. Course Requirements
- 15. Introduction to Dina's Dinner Party Case Study
- 17. Introduction Assignment

Chapter 1: Party Planning

- 20. Party Planning
- 20. The 8 A's of the Event Planning Process
- 21. Attire
- 21. Accessories
- 22. Anticipation
- 22. Arrival
- 23. Atmosphere
- 24. Appetite
- 25. Amusement
- 26. Appreciation
- 27. The Order of Party Planning
- 29. Case Study: Dina's Dinner Party A8 Planning
- 31. Chapter 1 Assignment

Chapter 2: Menu Planning

- 36. Choosing a Dinner Party Menu 101
- 39. Common Dinner Party Menus
- 40. Dinner Party Menu Planning
- 46. The Sensible Creation
- 53. Food & Wine Pairing
- 56. Dinner Party Menu Suggestions
- 57. Difficult Food & Wine Matches
- 59. Chapter 2 Assignment

Chapter 3: Table Design

- 62. Table Design
- 62. Table Linens
- 64. Tableware
- 71. Types of Crockery
- 76. Glassware
- 83. Chapter 3 Assignment

Chapter 4: Table Setting & Etiquette

- 86. Table Setting
- 86. Lay the Table Linen
- 87. Add the Centerpiece
- 88. Place the Cutlery
- 88. Place the Glassware
- 90. Add the Cruet Set, and any Accessories
- 90. Finally, the Chairs!
- 91. Stand Back and Admire the Smart Presentation
- 92. Table Etiquette
- 95. Chapter 4 Assignment

Chapter 5: Your Dinner Party Project

98. Project Content
98. Project Design
100. Dinner Party Time
102. Create the Menu
111. Wine and Drink Guide
113. Chapter 5 Assignment

Chapter 6: Dinner Party Project Planning

116. Dinner Party Planning
119. Dinner Party Vision
120. Mood Board Ideas
122. Hostess Tips
124. Plan the Concept
130. Madison's Dinner Party Planning and Design Details
140. Design and Plan Your Dinner Party
141. Chapter 6: Final Project
143. Mood Board Presentation
145. Glossary

INTRODUCTION

- Why Do We Entertain?
- Course Outline
- Course Navigation
- Course Goals & Objectives
- Course Requirements
- Introduction to Dina's Dinner Party Case Study
- Introduction Assignment

Why Do We Entertain?

You might ask yourself "Why do we entertain?" Truth is we could fill this whole book from cover to cover with different reasons, but for the sake of saving pages we will only talk about the most important ones.

One of the main reasons for entertaining is celebration. Celebration of life, milestones, and accomplishments are a great reason to gather our nearest and dearest to create beautiful lifetime memories.

Entertaining is also a way that we open our hearts and homes to those who we care for. Creating a worthwhile experience for our guests is key. By letting others into the most intimate part of our lives, we get to share our own personal style through the fun atmosphere we create, the food we serve, and the music we play.

On top of all this, hosting a party gets our creative juices flowing. From picking a theme to adding all of those little yet significant details, entertaining allows us to tap into our imagination and run wild with all of our ideas.

Overall, entertaining keeps us connected with others, allows us to channel our energetic and creative talents, and lets us share our personal style. Whatever the occasion, be it intimate or elaborate, just always remember the most important part is having fun with it!

Course Outline

Dina Manzo's series of party planning courses outline the fundamental formula for planning any event. From accessories to thank you notes and all the planning in-between, Dina teaches a DIYer how to stylize any event using practical, everyday items to mix and match your own signature style.

The course also covers food and wine pairing along with table setting etiquette, something many new DIYers may need a refresher on. Students will also learn how to select a menu and recognize what flavors of food and wine go best together.

COURSE NAVIGATION

- To navigate through this interactive course, students will use this book along with a student member account at:

    www.WeddingPlanningInstitute.com

- A password will be provided for students to login and access the online student center to watch instructional videos, download course tools, templates, and designs.

- Students will also have access to other students around the world in the online campus. Students can participate in discussions, share designs, photos of projects, and learn from a community of party planning peers.

- Each chapter has a quiz that is accessible in the student center. CEU's and points are automatically calculated after each quiz for review.

- A certificate of completion is generated once all course requirements are met. Students can print a certificate right from their membership profile page.

COURSE GOALS & OBJECTIVES

- Course goal: To learn the formulas, processes, roles and responsibilities of party planning.
- Target market: Anyone who wants the knowledge of how to plan for a social event.
- Course duration: An interactive short course, approximately eight hours.
- Course objectives: To provide the knowledge and examples of how to plan a perfect party, then execute that plan with a team of professional vendors and project manager (party planner).
- Course outcome: Understand the A8 planning formula used by professionals to design and plan a dinner party.

COURSE REQUIREMENTS

In this course students will learn how to design, plan and execute a dinner party. Case studies will be used to illustrate how the lessons and formulas relate to the outcome and results of a specific event.

To achieve the certificate of completion, students should:

- Read through the curriculum and watch the training videos that accompany each chapter.
- Use the lessons, assignments, and case studies to create a project plan and mood board using the formulas, methods, and techniques to plan and design a dinner party celebration. Students will grade themselves as there is no assignment submission. Each chapter's worksheet is located in the resource library.
- Complete the end of chapter quizzes located in the student center.

Introduction to Dina Manzo's Dinner Party Case Study

Dina Manzo is hosting 10 guests, a mixture of both friends and new associates, at a home in Calistoga, the Palazzo Della Montagna located in the wine country of Northern California. Students will learn by example and walk through the details of this event, along with the planning process, dinner menu, and table design.

Case Study Introduction

Who: Dina Manzo

What: Semi-formal dinner party

Where: A home, Palazzo Della Montagna, located in Calistoga, CA, in the outside loggia

When: Mid-Autumn, evening

Why: Celebrating new business friendships and new projects

How: Using Dina's party planning formulas, methods, and event styling techniques

Theme: Outdoor Autumn celebration of new book

Menu

- A salad of bibb lettuce, herbs and grained mustard
- Room temperature tomato soup, roasted salsa with chicory, truffle and olive oil
- Seared scallops and maine lobster with green curry, braised mushrooms, celery root and potatoes
- French toast with caramelized walnut 'ice cream' and maple syrup

10 Guests

Rental Requirements:

- 10 chargers - large decorative underplates
- 10 12" soup bowls with lip
- 10 10" salad plates
- 10 12" dinner plates
- 10 10" dessert bowls with lip
- 10 bread plates
- 10 knives
- 10 salad forks
- 10 dinner forks
- 10 soup spoons
- 10 dessert spoons
- 10 butter knives
- 10 red wine glasses
- 10 white wine glasses
- 10 champagne glasses
- 10 water glasses
- 4 water pitchers
- 15 napkins
- 2 bread baskets

Each table setting should consist of:

- Napkin
- Charger
- 1 bread plate with butter knife
- 1 knife
- 1 dinner fork
- 1 spoon
- 1 salad fork
- 1 dessert spoon
- 1 water glass
- 1 champagne glass
- 1 red wine glass
- 1 white wine glass

Introduction Assignment

Become familiar with the process of identifying the foundation of a celebration. Most celebrations have special meaning and purpose. Use the five "w" rule of who, what, where, when, and why, to pull together the purpose and objective for any special gathering. By identifying the five w's you can begin to apply the following lessons to design, plan, and deliver a perfect celebration. Visit the online Resource Library to download this worksheet.

Who: (the person hosting the party/event)

What: (the kind of party/event being hosted)

Where: (the location and setting of the event)

When: (the time, date, and season of the event)

Why: (the reason/importance of the event)

Chapter 1: Party Planning

- Party Planning
- The 8 A's of the Event Planning Process
- Attire
- Accessories
- Anticipation
- Arrival
- Atmosphere
- Appetite
- Amusement
- Appreciation
- The Order of Party Planning
- Case Study: Dina's Dinner Party A8 Planning
- Chapter 1 Assignment

Party Planning

When we plan a party we tend to focus on the menu, table setting, decorations and music. But our first consideration should be the guests; after all they are the real reason for the party.

Plan the guests list and how many will be invited. This will be based on available space and cooking facilities. Remember to accommodate the guests, so a space that is too crowded will not be comfortable.

It's important to pay attention to the guests' individual personalities. In a perfect setting, every guest would get along great and conversation would flow throughout the evening. However, keep in mind that this is not always the case.

Decide on who will make the best conversation with others, who will dance, and who will participate in the activities you have planned.

Careful planning requires attention to detail. If the party is well planned it will be stress free during the event. Writing all the details down on a party planning schedule (or diary) helps to keep track of all the tasks that need to be accomplished. A good way to confirm nothing is missed is to visualize the party from start to end. Walk through it step-by-step and fill in the details. Assigning a timeline and deadline to complete each of the associated tasks for the event helps to keep the planning organized and on schedule.

Dina Says:
You can keep the diary as a guideline for your next party and just change out the details.

A8 Party Planning & Design

Here we are going to walk through the A8 recipe of planning and designing for an event:

1. Attire.
2. Accessories.
3. Anticipation.
4. Arrival.
5. Atmosphere.
6. Appetite.
7. Amusement.
8. Appreciation.

Attire

As the "dress" and "code of dress" are key components of an event, they actually dictate the design features of the occasion. For a wedding, decisions about color and style set the scene when designing the entire event. For other party functions, as the host or hostess you might like to coordinate what you wear with a theme or the formality of the occasion. After all, you will be the center of attention, so embrace the situation.

It might be fun, when planning a party to send out invitations. If you are creating a theme, ask your guests to dress accordingly. Your guidelines could be as simple as "semi-formal attire will be appreciated" to something more challenging like "this is a purple party, so use your inventive talents and wear your best purple creation."

Accessories

What comes to mind when hearing the word accessories are the little details added to your attire that complete your whole look. Jewelry, hats, shoes, and handbags are all included in this list. Adding accessories to your outfit will enhance whatever you choose to wear; here is where it is possible to go crazy with detail. Careful coordination of fashion accessories often draws the comment "she thought of every little detail."

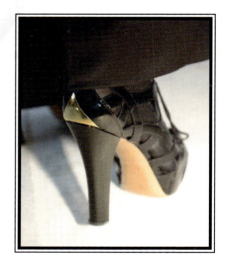

When it comes to party planning, accessories are the little "extras" or special touches that help create the overall look and feel of the party. The range is enormous, but the obvious ones include flowers, table and room decorations, candles, or gifts. Often times it is a nice added detail to include heirloom jewelry as part of the table setting and décor, such as cameos and broaches for napkin rings, as it adds to the interest and fun.

As the meal is often the main feature of the party, well planned accessories to the meal include the table setting. Careful consideration must be given to the table linen, china, flatware, cutlery and glassware used for your table setting.

Anticipation

The invitation is the first impression of any event and the first opportunity to capture a guest's curiosity for what you are planning and build his/her anticipation to attend. Anticipation is created by the nature and style of the invitation. Invitations can be sent out by a phone call, an email or our favorite, good old-fashioned postal service. The experience of opening an invitation to a special event is not to be over looked. It is this very moment that you start to generate excitement for your party. Selection of the design, color, and paper all play a role in the impression that is forming while your invitation is being opened. Go online and look at various invitation designs. If your budget allows for it, make sure you match the invitation style with place names, party programs and menu cards. The wording and font on the invitations should be carefully chosen: casual and chatty for informal occasions and precise for formal occasions.

With anticipation comes intrigue. Try and develop some intrigue when designing your party. Make your chosen guests want to be part of your personal celebration. Choosing a theme often makes the party planning process much easier because you can use it as your own inspiration when deciding on the design of the venue and the food and drink you will serve.

Arrival

There is a saying in the hospitality industry: "First impressions are the most lasting impressions." Certainly first impressions set the tone for the occasion and will last the rest of the event.

When planning your party, give special thought to how you would like your guests to arrive. Let the entrance match the style of the occasion. They might arrive in their own cars, but you have planned to have valet service greet them. If the distance from the parking lot to the venue is more than a few blocks, arrange for a golf cart to transport guests to and from the parking lot. Many guests will be dressed in their best attire, and walking a distance may be an uncomfortable experience. The choices are many, ranging from hiring a charter bus (for a crowd), a boat across the water, being dropped by a helicopter or hot-air balloon, or rambling in on foot!

As part of the entertainment for the party, a scenic tour and chat to absorb the moment before arriving at the party is a great way to get everyone connected.

You might also consider organizing the transportation for any out-of-town guests. It provides them with a stress free arrival in unfamiliar surroundings.

Atmosphere

Atmosphere is about feeling. It is created by the senses and the emotions. It is what people smell, see, hear, taste and touch, bound by how comfortable they feel in the presence of others. The hostess helps to create atmosphere. A warm and friendly welcome allows guests to bond with the occasion in a subtle and valuable way.

Atmosphere and comfort are connected. The amount of personal space given to guests at a party is an important consideration. If the space is too crowded, inner tensions develop and discomfort sets in. Be sure your space can comfortably accommodate the number of people invited to attend, including any planned activities.

Lighting not only creates mood, but also gives focus when required. Candles provide very intimate and relaxing lighting when dining. Uplighting is often used at parties. This is where LED lights are placed on the ground facing the walls or elements within the room that require illumination for special effects. Technically it requires a lighting expert, who will be able to create the desired effect. Static lighting is best during food service, whereas faded, strobe or changing light provides an exciting effect for dancing.

Many people consider music to be a major part of the atmosphere. Choosing the right music and the way it is delivered can be a demanding process especially when the detail is added. It may be provided by a home entertainment system, a live band or a DJ!

APPETITE

Appetite is not just about food: it is about the passion and desire of the whole occasion, of which food plays a vital part.

The time of day and season will influence food ideas. Appetite is stimulated by a sensible timing of service. This means delaying food service enough to inspire the taste buds, or serving an aperitif to excite the palate. But be careful. An excess of alcohol may cause unwelcome results on an empty stomach.

The only golden rules about providing food at parties are:

- The food and style of service must fit with the theme and culture of the occasion. Having a clam bake or a barbecue is as appropriate for a beach party as a paella feast at a Spanish-inspired party.
- People are likely to have a drink or two to celebrate the occasion, so the food should be substantial enough to minimize the effect of alcohol.
- People have different tastes, so choices of foods are necessary, including vegetarian options for people who don't eat meat. Do not forget any special diet needs of your guests.
- Lavish presentations do not necessarily produce the "wow" factor. Simple foods presented elegantly are just as appealing.

- Choose the foods that are successfully prepared in advance and able to be cooked in bulk if large numbers of guests are expected. If delays are to be expected, delicate food presentations are likely to wilt with impatience.
- Polish up on your table setting etiquette. The table should be as attractive as the food.
- For large parties the logistics of DIY catering are demanding. Imagine preparing, cooking, serving and cleaning up, at the same time as trying to host the occasion. It is probably best to do the planning and preparation and get help with the rest. For a function involving family or close friends, don't be afraid to take advantage of their talents by assigning some of the menu preparation to them. Or plan to cater some of the more difficult food items and serve it in your own dishes. Hiring a caterer is sometimes less than buying all of the food and doing it yourself.
- Whenever you choose recipes you have never made before, practice them well in advance of the party. Try your table setting ideas at least a week beforehand so you can make last minute adjustments with time to spare.
- Champagne is a good celebration drink. Beer, wine, fruit punch, soda and mineral water are great basic standards. It is trendy (and expensive) to launch into cocktails, and if the budget permits, go for it! Always remember to encourage responsible drinking and prevent the post party hangovers. Great times are not measured in how much people drink.

Amusement

At the heart of a good party is some form of entertainment. It is important to ensure all guests get into the party mood with the right type of amusement. A dance is popular because it is interactive, promotes social mingling, and people can either choose to watch or get involved.

It is popular to have a dance floor at a party, but it is more important to choose a DJ with personality and insist on the right sound and volume to suit the occasion. A live band might be more expensive than a DJ, yet a good band will provide top entertainment, especially if the players are diverse in their delivery and have someone captivating on the microphone.

Tribute acts can provide a fun feature, but they have to be good quality. Other amusement ideas include involving your guests in party games or competitions, or hiring performers in traditional dance, comedy or magic.

When people enjoy themselves, there may be a lot of noise involved. Give consideration to others in close proximity to the venue and cause as little disruption as possible. If holding a party in a private residence, it is polite to inform all neighbors so they will be more comfortable about the occasion. Check with your city on noise ordinances and how late your party can go.

Appreciation

Appreciation is part of the lasting impressions made after the party is over. Successful parties require appreciation to be a two-way street. The guests will appreciate the hostess for hosting the occasion and in turn the hostess will earn appreciation for being part of the occasion.

Timing is one factor that earns appreciation. It is not good practice to abandon your guests to attend to one of the menu or decoration details you should have organized before they arrived. Tell yourself your party starts 30 minutes before it actually does, so you have time in store should something require your attention. If not, then relax and catch your breath before your guests arrive.

Lasting impressions are obtained by achieving excellence in the gold trio: food, company and comfort.

One of the best things to strive for when planning a party is achieving the "feel-good" factor, the collective feeling of well-being. Two of life's feel-good factors are connecting with friends and receiving compliments. These are synonymous with appreciation.

The Order of Party Planning

Put all your planning into order:

1. Begin with the guest list.
2. Design the perfect menu.
3. Match the food with the right wines (or beverages).
4. Add a dash of fun with entertainment.
5. Choose your music to suit the occasion.
6. Set the scene with proper lighting and creative table setting.
7. Be ready to be the best hostess.

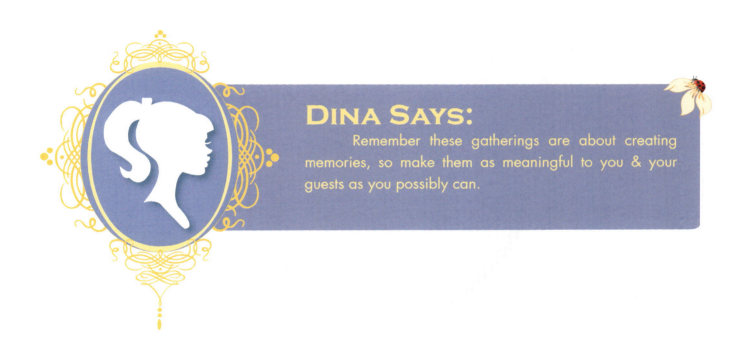

DINA SAYS:
Remember these gatherings are about creating memories, so make them as meaningful to you & your guests as you possibly can.

Case Study: Dina's Dinner Party A8 Planning

Outline of A8 usage in case study

Attire

Dina had many options she brought with her for the semi-formal dinner party. She selected a conservative, yet comfortable black dress. Being at home brings a sense of comfort so soft and easy fabrics work well.

She wore her hair in a loose, low and off center up-do to match the feel of the evening and atmosphere. A warm and comfortable space that is inviting and relaxing was the goal and her hairstyle matched the atmosphere she had set for the evening.

She decided on a natural look for her make-up with a pop of color for her lips. It has been said that red is a powerful lip color when you have something important to say.

Accessories

Dina chose to wear small earrings with a multilayered necklace, a bracelet and cocktail ring. All accessories were in the same color family of gold and complemented her blond hair and black dress.

Anticipation

An impromptu dinner party didn't give Dina enough time to design or select an invitation to be mailed to her guests as she would normally plan. Instead, a personal phone call was placed to invited guests.

To create excitement and anticipation pictures of the venue and details of the event were emailed along with a guest itinerary.

Arrival

Travel to the venue was required by all attendees, so directions and maps were sent to the guests electronically. The special guests of honor were transported by car service from the airport to the venue location.

Upon arrival, guests were greeted as they drove in and escorted into the home. Bags and any items needing to be carried in were taken care of by the house's caretaker.

Atmosphere

As guests approached and entered the location, ambient style music could be heard and the aromas from the kitchen filled the air. The home was decorated beautifully by its owners Tim and Gene. The architectural details were painstakingly built over several years, with historical elements from around the world. Using this amazing canvas to plan a dinner party was not difficult as the surroundings provided a constant curiosity of design details from the ceilings, walls, floors, lighting, and furniture.

Additional décor was brought in for the dinner party table to complement the surroundings in the home and the theme of the evening. Using a color palette of soft blues, gold, ivory and cream, the linens were chosen to offer a base to the color palette for the event and the backdrop/canvas to the tablescape.

Dina decided to mix outdoor elements with traditional table settings by adding grapevine and cabbage leaves to the floral centerpieces. The guests had many items on the table to explore and touch with many textures, heights, and colors. A long and low centerpiece was created with various heights of tapered candles with ornate candle holders. Because the celebration was specific to a new business relationship and launching her new course, books were also incorporated into the long-low floral centerpiece design of the dinner table.

Votive candles were used throughout the outdoor room and on the table to set a warm and inviting atmosphere. The outdoor fireplace was also lit and provided warmth and ambiance on a crisp autumn evening.

The music continued to play through out the evening and provided a soft and relaxing vibe as guests enjoyed the conversations.

Appetite

The menu for the evening consisted of locally grown seasonal items:

- A Salad of Bibb Lettuce, Herbs and Grained Mustard
- Room Temperature Tomato Soup, Roasted Salsa with Chicory, Truffle and Olive Oil
- Seared Scallops and Maine Lobster with Green Curry, Braised Mushrooms, Celery Root and Potatoes
- French Toast with Caramelized Walnut "Ice Cream" and Maple Syrup

Amusement

Aside from the enjoyable new relationships and conversations going on that evening, Dina's dinner party guests were entertained by a famous local chef, Randall Selland, from The Selland's Group of Restaurants, such as "The Kitchen," "Ella's" and "Selland's Market Place." Chef Randall entertained the guests by walking through the menu for the evening and describing each course along with details on preparation. He also walked through the wine for the evening and assisted guests with the selection principles for food and wine pairing.

Appreciation

The timing of our event was soon after the Super Storm Sandy, a very difficult time for many people in the northeast of the United States. The A8 planning principles recommend a form of appreciation should follow every event. In many cases, a small favor is designed or purchased as a gift to each guest. For Dina's dinner party in Calistoga, a $1000 donation was sent to the American Red Cross to support the victims of Super Storm Sandy.

Chapter 1 Assignment

Create an outline of the A8 for a dinner party you plan to have. Visit the online Resource Library to download this worksheet.

Chapter 2: Menu Planning

- Choosing a Dinner Party Menu 101
- Common Dinner Party Menus
- Dinner Party Menu Planning
- The Sensible Creation
- Food & Wine Pairing
- Dinner Party Menu Suggestions
- Difficult Food & Wine Matches
- Chapter 2 Assignment

Choosing a Dinner Party Menu 101

Choosing a Menu for a Dinner Party 101

Start with the six Ws.

Who

- Who is the event for?
- Friends
- Dignitary
- Bride and Groom
- Do they have dietary restrictions?
- Allergies
- Religious beliefs
- Personal beliefs
- Do they drink?
- Are they foodies and/or do they love meat and potatoes
- Knowing who your guests are is very helpful.

What

- What is the purpose of the event?
- Wedding
- Business meeting
- Casual get together
- Formal dinner party
- Sit down dinner
- Buffet
- Family style
- The type of event will determine what to serve.

WHERE

- Where will the event be held?
- In a home
- At an event facility
- What is the kitchen like?
- Is it an open or closed kitchen?

WHEN

- When will the event be held?
- Morning
- Day
- Dinner hour
- Night
- What is the season?
- What products will be available?
- Should it be winter comfort food or light summer fair?

WHY

- Why is this event happening?
- Is this event a celebration?
- Is it to mourn or reflect?

WINE

- Wine is the final ingredient in any meal.
- Are your guests wine novices, experts or somewhere in between?
- Should you pair the wine with each course?

The Menu

The word "menu" comes from a Latin word "minutus" which means a detailed list. It was first found in print in France. If we take guidance in menu planning from the French, we would produce 17 courses for a classical (formal) French dinner. It does not amount to copious quantities of food though, because each course consists of a tasty morsel, well prepared and superbly presented. A modified classical menu consists of the following courses:

- Hors-d'oeuvre - Two or three tasty savories (or finger food) per person before a dinner. This may be served as well as, or instead of an entrée.
- Soup - A thick, thin or creamy broth with a meat, fish or vegetable base, often served instead of hors-d'oeuvres.
- Entrée - This should be light, appetizing and provocative. It is not the main course but should be complementary to the rest of the meal.
- Sorbet - A tangy and frozen fruit ice that cleanses the palate.
- Main course - The main event. It is good practice to plan other courses and beverages around the main course.
- Dessert - This should make the dinner feel satisfied. A heavy or spicy main course should be followed by a light fruity dessert.
- Cheese - In France, a cheese course will be served before dessert. Some people prefer savory to sweet tastes, therefore cheese is used as a substitute for dessert.
- Petits fours/friandises - For special occasions delicious truffles, chocolates or pastries provide a decadent touch alongside coffee.

All of the aforementioned courses may be offered in a very formal meal today, but usually modern menus consist of 3-4 courses built around foods that are in season.

It is not necessary to include exotic or unique ingredients. However, one might be inspired by a single culinary culture, or in the case of fusion food, a blend of culinary cultures. An example of this is Pacific Rim food which combines the spices of East Asian countries, the tropical fruits of the Pacific Islands and fresh fish and vegetables from the American coast.

Common Dinner Party Menus

Menu examples of the four most common courses:

Soup

Examples of cold soup:

- Vichyssoise
- Gazpacho

Examples of hot soup:

- Cream of vegetable
- Seafood chowder
- Lobster bisque
- Chicken and corn soup
- Consommé

Entrée

An entrée is sometimes called a "starter" in a 3-course menu and usually consists of a single food item served hot with a sauce. It is not a substantial meal, but medium-sized, and not accompanied by vegetables unless as a garnish.

Menu examples of an entrée:

- Grilled mussels with sweet Thai chili sauce
- Vegetarian wontons with a gingered soy dipping sauce
- Chicken liver and cognac pâté with toasted bruschetta
- Pan fried pork loin chop with a guava gin sauce

The main course

A simple main course consists of a meat, fish, poultry or other protein food, served with one or two vegetables and potatoes (or bread, rice or pasta). The main component is usually served with a hot or cold sauce, or gravy.

Menu examples of a bmain course:

- Chicken roasted with thyme butter, grilled chilies, eggplant and sweet corn
- Lamb rump cooked pink, and served with roast aubergine and courgette
- Casseroled beef rump with winter root vegetables
- Salmon fillet baked with prosciutto and mushrooms on a bed of crispy noodles

Dessert

Other terms for dessert are "sweet," "afters" or "pudding."

The dessert course can include:

- Hot dishes, such as crumbles and sweet pastries
- Cold desserts such as pavlova, cheesecake, bavarois, fresh fruit salad

Menu examples of dessert:

- Cream sponge with blueberries, lemon honey and whipped cream
- Chocolate mousse
- Tiramisu
- Baked apricot tartlets

Dinner Party Menu Planning

The principles of menu planning are the same, whether cooking for the family or wanting to impress with entertainment. You need to strive for balance, emphasize variety, and produce contrasts of color that produce eye appeal. But before we launch into "good practices" remember two things:

1. Simple is often best.
2. Fresh is always best.

A successful meal is tasty, palatable and satisfying. The secrets underlying this successful meal are in the planning. Good menu planning is all about achieving balance, not only in nutrients, but also in color, texture, flavor, ingredients and cooking methods.

A BALANCE OF NUTRIENTS

No, you do not need to be a dietitian, but if you get this balance right you are well on the way to achieving good color, texture and variety in the meal. To aim for nutritional balance, it is important to include foods from each food group. The protein (meat, fish, eggs or cheese) is usually the hero of the dish, and the vegetables (providing vitamins and minerals) are the accompaniment, while the carbohydrate (potato, rice, pasta, bread) is the filler.

People watching their weight will want to eliminate the carbohydrates, but we need them for energy and without them we may not feel satisfied at the end of the meal.

A BALANCE OF COLOR

There is a saying "we eat with our eyes" and it is true when we see an attractive combination of colors of food on a plate. Imagine this: pan-fried crumbed fish, potato chips, cauliflower with white sauce and braised onions. Where is the color?

If you wish to serve fish with vegetables, a more attractive combination would be: pan-fried crumbed fish with lemon butter and garnished with a sprig of parsley, red potato slices, broccoli and grilled tomato halves. Let's tag this menu while we explore the following balancing factors.

A BALANCE OF TEXTURE

A variety of textures satisfies the palate. If all items on the plate are soft and smooth, they do not challenge the palate. Our palate likes soft, smooth, succulent, crisp, liquid and grainy textures, but is not fond of tough, stringy, dry, gluey, greasy and furry textures in food.

Returning to the fish meal, we have pan-fried crumbed fish (crisp) with lemon butter (smooth) and garnished with a sprig of parsley (crisp), red potato slices (crisp and grainy), broccoli (soft) and grilled tomato halves (soft). The texture can be varied by substituting the broccoli and tomatoes with a garden fresh salad.

A BALANCE OF FLAVOR

A meal is superb if it can excite the taste buds. There are four basic flavor sensations: sweet, sour, salty and bitter. There are also numerous other flavor descriptions, such as spicy, hot, mellow, herbal, aromatic, fruity, savory and smoky. A careful combination of these can be complementary, but if the meal is dominated by one flavor sensation only, the taste buds will not be stimulated. Let's test the fish meal for flavor: pan-fried crumbed fish with lemon butter and garnished with a sprig of parsley, red potato slices, broccoli and grilled tomato halves. There is a combination of salt, sour, herbal and slightly bitter flavors.

A BALANCE OF COOKING METHODS

Color, texture and flavor are influenced by the method of cooking used. Frying coats all food with fat therefore tends to produce crisp (slightly greasy) food. Boiling and steaming generally produces bland, soft food. Baking, grilling and roasting add a crust and flavor to the surface, and a softness to the center of the food. If all foods on the menu were cooked by the same method, you also run the risk of running out of cooking space. Cooking pasta, pasta sauce, and pan-fried or boiled vegetables all require the stove top. Replacing the boiled vegetables with a salad, relieves the stove top and provides a better texture balance to the meal. Let's test the fish meal for cooking methods: pan-fried crumbed fish (shallow frying) with lemon butter and garnished with a sprig of parsley, red potato slices (deep frying or oven baking), broccoli (boiling) and grilled tomato halves (grilling). This represents a really good balance.

Included in this section is a balance of foods that can be prepared (or even cooked) ahead of time, to foods that require last-minute cooking. If all the items on your menu required last minute cooking, be prepared for bedlam!

A balance of main food items, including ingredients

Avoid repetition of the same food when planning a menu. It is best to give a bad example of a 3-course menu to illustrate what this means:

- Entree: deep fried camembert with cranberry sauce.
- Main course: broccoli and bacon tagliatelle with shaved parmesan, served with green salad.
- Dessert: tangy citrus and mango cheesecake.

You have spotted it already; cheese at every course and hopefully the green salad does not have a feta cheese garnish!

Apart from the main food items, a variety of ingredients within the recipes is essential. A dominant flavor has slipped into this menu: pork noodle soup with cinnamon and anise; followed by lamb tagine with prunes and cinnamon; then for dessert, fruit kebabs coated with brown sugar, cinnamon and honey.

Yes, cinnamon adds spice, depth and warmth to food, and is even believed to reduce blood sugar levels. All that aside, it should not be allowed to dominate the taste buds.

Start with the best ingredients. Fresh is best, so make the most of fresh and seasonal local ingredients because they are plentiful, at their best and therefore cheaper to put on the menu. Frozen and tinned products do not present as well. Generally the process of preservation alters the texture and color of foods, making them less desirable than fresher alternatives. As an example, if you intend to make a fresh berry tart, the tinned alternatives will not have the same eye appeal.

The Sensible Creation

The menu must be sensible and achievable by those working in the kitchen. A menu that is too complicated for the skills of the cooks will not succeed. The quality of the food far outweighs your efforts to show off a complicated recipe that is difficult to match the illustration provided.

Plan the order, then the final symphony:

1. Begin with the main course because it is the primary feature of the meal, and therefore the most complex and substantial dish in the menu. This is usually the most expensive item on the menu, therefore it should be given the respect it deserves.

2. Plan the preceding courses (hors d'oeuvres and entrée) to prepare your guests for the main course. Don't let them compete with the main course. Think of them as a "prelude to the main act."

3. Finish with a memorable dessert. This doesn't mean something that is lavish and creamy. Technically, everything after the main course should calm the stomach and the senses. If earlier courses are rich, it will be exhausting to finish with the high-end of calories. A light and fruity dessert is more complementary and better for digestion.

We eat with our eyes. The food we like to eat in cafés and restaurants is not the same as what we cook at home. It should be different, although parties are a good way to introduce a new ingredient or new combinations of other ingredients that you wouldn't normally use for dinner. If you are confident, introduce an element of surprise in a dish, but do not throw all the principles of good menu planning out the window in the process.

How the food is presented is also part of the experience. The goal in constructing a menu is presenting your guests with food that sounds good, tastes great, and makes them truly satisfied.

EXAMPLE:

We will put all the above menu planning principles into an example. Say you wish to plan a three-course meal for an early summer dinner party for ten guests. You have decided on a Moroccan theme so you wish to feature Moroccan spiced lamb with aubergine and couscous for the main course. Take note the flavors in the dish:

Menu	Recipe	Main ingredients and flavors	Accompaniments
Soup/Entrée			
Main course	Moroccan spiced lamb with aubergine and couscous	Lamb, ginger, turmeric, pepper, cinnamon, cumin, aubergine, garlic, tomato	Couscous, currants, almonds, coriander
Dessert			

This is certainly a strong Middle Eastern statement made for the main course. The best thing you can do now is stay with this and research other flavors used in Moroccan cookery, thus you will see Moroccans are big meat eaters. You might have the traditional Kebab Koutbane for an entrée, which features small cubes of spiced beef fillet steak, grilled or barbecued. Since already having a spicy main course, we've decided on a dish that prepares the guests for this course:

Menu	Recipe	Main ingredients and flavors	Accompaniments
Soup/Entrée	Moroccan carrot soup crispy flatbread	Carrot, chicken stock, onion, lime juice, chopped parsley	Crispy flat bread
Main course	Moroccan spiced lamb with aubergine and couscous	Lamb, ginger, turmeric, pepper, cinnamon, cumin, aubergine, garlic, tomato	Couscous, currants, almonds, coriander
Dessert			

Now for the dessert. When you think of Morocco, think of halva (a dense sweet made of semolina, sesame paste and sunflower seeds), or coconut fudge cake. As both of these might be too complex after such a spicy main course, it is best to feature seasonal fruit that will cleanse the taste buds. We need to think of a way to make the fruit exciting in order to achieve a memorable finish:

Menu	Recipe	Main ingredients and flavors	Accompaniments
Soup/Entrée	Moroccan carrot soup crispy flatbread	Carrot, chicken stock, onion, lime juice, chopped parsley	Crispy flat bread
Main course	Moroccan spiced lamb with aubergine and couscous	Lamb, ginger, turmeric, pepper, cinnamon, cumin, aubergine, garlic, tomato	Couscous, currants, almonds, coriander
Dessert	Circle oranges	Oranges, strawberries, in Cointreau, topped with chopped pistachio nuts	Cinnamon and sugar

Moroccans tend to drink green tea with mint as an accompaniment to their meal. This would complement beautifully with all courses, especially the lamb. But if you wish to serve wine, your best option would be a Shiraz (Syrah) or Merlot.

Now we will test the menu for balance:

Balance	Examples
Nutrients	Protein (chicken stock, lamb, almonds, pistachio nuts) Carbohydrates (couscous, flat bread) Vitamins and minerals (carrots, lime, parsley, aubergine, tomato, oranges, strawberries)
Color	Soup (orange, green garnish and golden flat bread) Main course (brown meat, purple aubergine, red tomato, golden white couscous with green capsicum) Dessert (orange and red fruit with green pistachio and brown cinnamon)
Texture	Soup (liquid) Flatbread (crisp) Lamb (soft) Couscous (grainy and crisp) Oranges, strawberries and pistachio (soft and crisp)
Flavor	Soup (herbal, tangy poultry flavor) Main course (spicy, herbal, slightly bitter meat flavor, sweet herbal couscous) Dessert (tangy and sweet alcohol)
Cooking methods	Soup (boiling, baking) Main course (shallow frying, braising, steaming) Dessert (toasting, if sugar and cinnamon are glazed)
Food items	No repetition

It appears to be a perfectly balanced menu, providing it meets the satisfaction of the guests. Of course, individual tastes will dictate individual levels of satisfaction, but at least you can say:

- For early summer most of the ingredients are seasonal, therefore should be fresh.
- The menu features good quality food to satisfy a moderate budget.
- The menu is simple and the courses do not require professional expertise.
- The slightly tangy carrot/lime flavored soup is good preparation for the spicy complex lamb, aubergine and tomato main course.
- After such a complex main course, the dessert refreshes the palate and provides a memorable touch by adding an orange liqueur.
- The flavor combinations in each course provide an element of surprise.

ACTIVITY: PLAN YOUR OWN MENU

You are about to plan a four course dinner menu for a party. You have decided on oriental salmon served on a bed of stir-fried noodles and a garden-fresh green salad for the main course. Plan the other courses to go with this course. Visit the online Resource Library to download this worksheet.

Menu	Recipe	Main ingredients and flavors	Accompaniments
Hors D'oeuvres or soup			
Entrée			
Main course	Oriental salmon	Baked salmon fillet with garlic, lemongrass, ginger, soy sauce, coriander	Stir-fried udon noodles, spring onions, honey, soy sauce Lettuce, diced tomato, cucumber and toasted sesame seed salad
Dessert			

Now, check for balance:

Balance	Examples
Nutrients	
Color	
Texture	
Flavor	
Cooking methods	
Food items	

Planning a menu providing a choice of food

When DIY catering for a multi-course dinner party, it is very rare to offer the guests a choice of food like that offered in an a la carte restaurant. When you wish to allow guests a choice of food, a buffet meal is a sensitive alternative.

Buffet service is a form of self-service from a pre-set table. There can be many variations of buffet service, but the three main ones are:

1. Sit down buffets, where guests select their meal from the buffet table(s) and eat it at dining tables that may be pre-set.
2. Fork buffets, where guests stand to eat and the type of food is easily eaten with a fork, such as curries and rice dishes.
3. Finger food buffets, where guests receive a plate and approach the buffet table from several points to select their food.

There are hot buffets, cold buffets, salad bars and dessert tables. Buffets can be either casual or semi-formal. They provide a more relaxed method of dining and have the advantage of allowing guests to inspect the food before selecting it. Buffet service is used anytime there are large gatherings, even at many formal wedding receptions.

The same basic menu planning principles when providing a choice of foods apply, but be careful when you are planning with variety.

When offering a choice of four main course dishes, make sure you don't choose a repeat of the same main ingredients. A good basic choice is: one red meat, one white meat, one fish dish, and one vegetarian dish.

Salads should not be all from the same food group, like carbohydrate. Imagine if your choice of salads were potato salad, rice salad, pasta salad and couscous. Here is an example of a good choice:

- Roast vegetable salad
- Lettuce and rocket salad
- Tomato and avocado salad
- Carrot, pineapple and raisin salad
- Tabbouleh (bulgur, cucumber, parsley, mint and lemon salad)

The same applies to dessert. Do not make a table full of the same types of desserts, like sweet pies. Do not make all the desserts with cream. A good variety would include:

- One gateau
- One fresh fruit dish
- One creamy dish (such as a bavarois or cheese cake)
- Another type, such as fruit crumble, meringue or jelly

Food & Wine Pairing

Matching the Food with the Wine

You may have heard the basic no-nonsense color coordinated statement "red wine goes with red meat, white wine with white meat." This provided a good "rule" when food options and wine styles were simple.

Today, we have a wealth of food options and vast range of wine styles to choose from. We have borrowed strong spices from other cuisines where traditionally they do not drink wine with their food. So, in some ways the above statement no longer exists, but is a good starting point. It won't solve the problem of what to drink with "pan fried fillet of pork with baby langoustine, onion lyonnaise and a light madeira jus." This has red meat and seafood in the same dish!

Do not treat food and wine matching as an exact science. At the same time you should not adopt the attitude of "anything goes." When connoisseurs advise on the choice of beverage that will match the menu item, they consider the following characteristics of the food:

- Temperature
- Texture
- Intensity of flavor

Then they look for compatible characteristics of the wine:

Characteristics of Food	Characteristics of Wine
Temperature	Temperature
Texture	Mouthfeel
Intensity of flavor: - Salty, piquant, spicy etc. - Sweetness - Richness - Subtleness	Taste characteristics: - Fruit (cherries, lemon, raspberry etc.) - Savory (oak, nut, smoke, earthy) - Body or alcohol content (low 9-11%: medium 12-13%: high 13% +) - Sugar/acid/tannin

Looks daunting, but at the heart of the subject there are four helpful suggestions:

- Match the intensity of flavors in food and wine:
  - Strong flavored foods with strong flavored wines. A tannic wine, such as Cabernet Sauvignon can complement a full flavored meat such as roast beef, venison or game.
  - Light flavored foods with light-flavored wines. A light dry white wine, acidic fruit juice or a light lager will complement shellfish and lighter white fish.
  - Moist cooking methods (stews) produce intense rich flavors, therefore they should be matched with complex full-flavored wines. However, if you are serving chicken (delicate flavor) braised in a red wine sauce (strong flavor), then it is appropriate to match this dish with a red wine.
  - Dry cooking methods (grills) for finer textured food. If accompanying sauce is light in flavor intensity, match it with a light-flavored wine.
  - Poached dishes are usually delicate, therefore should be teamed with a light, young white wine.
- Match the sweetness levels in the food and wine:
  - Pair dry wines with savory foods and medium wines with sweeter tasting dishes.
  - Sweetness in a dish can come from the richness of the meat or the vegetables and sauce it is served with.
  - Sweet desserts with late harvest wines. Be careful. Sweetness of food can be buried under spices and will therefore disguise the natural food flavors. Seasonings, sauces, marinades and dressings can introduce a number of different flavors to a dish.
- Match one or two similar flavors:
  - Pick one or two dominant flavors in the food and match these with like flavors in the wine.
  - A good example is a mature Pinot Noir (with its notable earthy flavors) with mushroom soup.
  - Consider the body or weight of the wine.
- Match the body or weight of the wine with the food:
  - A wine's body or weight corresponds closely with it's alcoholic strength, so try to match a wine's body to the power of the strongest ingredient in the food.
  - Serve delicate-flavored foods such as poached chicken with lighter bodied wines or grape juice.
  - Stronger, more robust foods such as grilled tuna, veal or pork dishes should be served with full-bodied wines.

When planning an important celebration, take time to taste the food and wine combination to make sure they work together.

Drinking several wines throughout the menu

Gone are the days when we drank the same wine from the beginning to the end of a meal at a dinner party. Did you ever wonder why that delicious dessert that you labored over tasted so ordinary when it came time to eat it? It was probably because you still had half a glass of Cabernet Sauvignon to finish. Changing wine as you change the course is called a "wine flight" and makes a menu so much more interesting. The change complements the menu and helps the diner to focus on the different tastes that the meal and the wines create.

Ideally the match between the menu and the wines should not overwork the palate but allow a careful progression. It you start drinking Shiraz or a powerful Cabernet Sauvignon as an apéritif, every wine that follows will taste dull and ordinary. A big, full-bodied wine can leave your palate exhausted and lacking sensitivity to more subtle flavors. It is best to work up to these wines and start off with something more aromatic and invigorating. Below are some suggested food and wine pairing tips to start things off right:

- The herbaceous, zesty Sauvignon Blanc can be so fresh and fruity that it is difficult to match with subtle food. It is, however, an excellent apéritif with robustly flavored canapés or tapas (spinach roulade, goats cheese, greenshell mussels).
- Ripe, heavily oaked Chardonnay is often full of toasted nuts, vanillin and caramel flavors that make it difficult to match with delicate fish or chicken dishes.
- Food with considerable fat content such as deep fried battered fish, should be matched with a dry wine with good acidity.
- A deliciously fruity full-bodied Shiraz with its velvet mouth feel is a great match for strong flavored meats and sauces.
- A fruit-driven Pinot Noir, full of dark cherries and raspberries can equally balance a hearty meat course.
- An elegant Pinot Noir with less primary fruit characteristics and more savory oak can provide the perfect balance to new season's lamb.
- Spicy foods are best with a Gewürztraminer, or steer away from wine and choose beer.
- A sweet dessert will taste sweeter if paired with a dry wine. At the same time the wine will taste drier and more acidic, therefore is not a good match. The sweet white wines, particularly those made from 'noble rot' grapes are a good recommendation for the sweet course.
- Ports and sweet dessert wines are so rich and intense they can withstand the savory, tangy characteristics of cheese.
- With coffee, digestif spirits and liqueurs may be recommended.

Dinner Party Menu Suggestions

Menu items explained	A good wine match
Tapas or canapés: sweet shrimp with feta and cucumber	Method Traditionelle
Calamari with arugula, tomatoes and bacon on walnut sourdough	Sauvignon Blanc
Grilled crayfish with avocado, smoked bacon and sherry vinaigrette	Chardonnay, dry Pinot Gris, dry Riesling
Rare tuna with fresh ginger and lemon-grass dressing	Off-dry Riesling, Pinot Gris
Sautéed scallops on udon noodles with ponzu dressing	Gewürztraminer
Seared pork filet with prosciutto, spinach and golden brown butter	Rosé
Roasted rack of Canterbury lamb with caramelized cauliflower, capers, golden raisins, pinot-reduced pan juices	Pinot Noir
Braised lamb shank in rich tomato broth with grilled onion and garlic aioli	Merlot
Prime fillet of beef with Swiss chard, thyme, Armagnac-green peppercorn sauce	Shiraz
Meyer lemon tart with orange-scented sorbet	Asti
Crème caramel with poached apricots and nougatine	Noble Riesling

Difficult Food & Wine Matches

Few foods will actually "destroy wine," but some are tricky to match:

- Hot spicy foods tend to stun the taste buds and make it impossible to experience the subtle dimensions of wine, therefore beer or cider might be more appropriate.
- Some vegetables, such as asparagus or mushrooms, tend to make wine pairing difficult because of their distinctive flavors.
- Fish makes a tannin red wine taste metallic, and a savory dish with a sweet white wine can be very cloying.
- Care needs to be taken matching an egg dish with red wine because of the sulfur content in eggs.
- Acidic foods, such as tomatoes or vinaigrette dressing, are problematic with highly acidic wines.
- Peppermint flavors can destroy all abilities to detect wine characteristics.
- Rich chocolate, such as that in a mud cake, can be very mouth-coating, making it difficult to match with a wine.

Chapter 2 Assignment

Matching wine with food

Below is a three-course dinner party menu. Choose a wine to go with each of the courses provided and give your reasons for the match. Visit the online Resource Library to download this worksheet.

Menu	Description of food items in terms of flavor, temperature and taste characteristics	Choice of wine	Description of wine in terms of sweetness/dryness, body and taste characteristics
Entree	Brushetta with shrimp, tarragon mayonnaise and arugula, topped with mascarpone cheese and grilled		
Main course	Beef bourguignon with buttered new potatoes, garden fresh asparagus and grilled tomato halves		
Dessert	Lime parfait with melon sorbet, honeycomb and chocolate sauce		

Chapter 3: Table Design

- Table Design
- Table Linen
- Tableware
- Types of Crockery
- Glassware
- Chapter 3 Assignment

TABLE DESIGN

A meal is best when all components blend to create the magical ambiance. Delicious food should always be paired with beautiful table design, or else it just won't be quite the same. Adding special touches will make the occasion more personal and will awe your guests.

TABLE LINEN

Linen is a generic term referring to all material cloths, large and small used to dress a table (and sometimes chairs). Table linen includes table cloths, including skirts and overlays, slip cloths, table runners, placemats, napkins, buffet cloths, and wine cloths.

Table linen comes in a multitude of different colors, thicknesses, textures and patterns. Although referred to as "linen" there is a wide range of fabrics including Irish linen, satin, damask, cotton, sheer and brocades. More recently easily laundered polyester and viscose fabrics have been added to the range.

When beginning your table design, choose your cloth first. If the cloth has a pattern or color, make sure the slip cloth (or overlay), placemats and napkins do not have conflicting patterns.

TABLECLOTHS

Tablecloths are fabric covers used to cover the top and sides of the table. They can be round, square or rectangular or multi-sided to match the size of the table.

Tablecloths are used for the following reasons:

- Provide a contrasting background for the crockery
- Hide the table tops and legs
- Absorb heat and spillages
- Reduce noise

SLIP CLOTHS

A slip cloth is a small overlay cloth that is placed on top of an already placed tablecloth. It might be of contrasting color and is often placed at an angle to the main cloth.

Chair Covers

Chair covers are mostly used as part of the table design at weddings, but are just as effective at formal dinner parties. They can create a special effect or are valuable if your dining chairs are a little worn. Many companies have one-size-fits-all chair covers and a range of colors to choose from.

Table Runners

A table runner is a narrow strip cloth that is placed down the center of the table to place the table centerpiece and condiments on. It may be laid on a bare table top, or over the base cloth.

Placemats

Placemats are rectangular fabric mats to act as a base for each place setting.

They are a guide for the place setting and should be large enough to ensure the cutlery can be set to the outer edges with room for a main plate between the cutlery.

Placemats may sit directly on the table or over the tablecloth and can become an integral part of the table design.

Although paper is frowned upon when considering table linen, paper placemats are wonderful if you wish to personalize the occasion. Have them printed with "Happy Birthday Margie," "Congratulations Brad and Sophie," "Bon Voyage," or whatever the party is to celebrate.

Napkins

The napkins may be folded and placed, one for each guest, on the table as part of the table setting. They can be colored to match the theme and style of the table setting.

Wine Cloths

Generally a wine cloth is made of a fabric of equal quality to the napkins, although a spare napkin is just as good as it is clean and free from lint. Wine cloths are used to:

- Carry items (such as cutlery) to the table
- Wipe the neck of a wine bottle when opening and pouring wine
- Hold over the top of a sparkling wine bottle to avoid the cork flying out
- Cover an ice bucket
- Give cutlery or glassware a last-minute polish

Tableware

Cutlery, Flatware and Hollow-ware

1. Cutlery and Flatware

Technically, "cutlery" refers to knives and all cutting implements, while "flatware" is all forms of spoons and forks and serving platters. Today we refer to all eating implements (knives, spoons and forks) as cutlery and flatware as all flat plates.

For traditional and formal table settings these items are silver plated. There are different grades of silver and each item will have a number on it relating to the life time expected from the plating. The larger the number, the heavier the item because of the weight of the silver deposit. Although polished silver looks spectacular, it is very time-consuming to maintain, is easily stained and is likely to scratch with constant use.

Stainless steel cutlery and flatware is readily available today because of its versatility and ease of handling and washing. It is available in various grades and is finished by different degrees of polishing. Stainless steel can be high polish, dull polish, or matte and non-reflective finish. It does not scratch or tarnish as readily as silver.

Main Knife

The main knife has a blunt tip and usually has a slight serration to assist with cutting meat used for all main course items (except fish or steak).

Steak Knife

A steak knife has a sharp serrated blade to cut through steaks easily in a saw-like action. Strict care is needed when handling the sharp blade (during washing and polishing). Non-slip handles are often part of the steak knife design to reduce slippage when cutting a steak.

Fish or entrée knife

The fish or entrée knife has a blade that is blunt and rounded, suitable for portioning fish. Because of the shape of this knife it is also used as an entrée knife when soft or delicate foods are served, such as omelets, pâté or terrine.

Specialized Tableware

Cake Slice

The cake slice is sometimes called a pastry slice and is designed to cut and lift a portion of cake onto a plate.

The edge of the slice is used for cutting and separating the portions of cake. The blade of the slice is wedge shaped to hold a similar shaped piece of cake or pie.

Oyster Fork

The prongs of an oyster fork are sharp to pierce the skin around the oyster. With a twist and scoop action the oyster is held firmly and lifted out of the shell or dish.

It differs from the entrée fork because it has 3 prongs rather than 4 prongs. The prongs are sharper and sometimes barbed.

Butter Knife

The butter knife is regarded as an "old-fashioned" piece of equipment today. It is shaped like a mini fish knife and is used to lift butter portions from the butter plate onto the side plate. Strict, old-fashioned etiquette prevented it from being used to spread the butter on the bread.

Today we tend to use side knives for this purpose.

Sauce Ladle

The sauce ladle accompanies the sauce boat. The ladle has a deep bowl and the sides are shaped to pour evenly over the food item.

Nut Crackers

Slight pressure on the handles (closing in on the nut) will allow the nut cracker to break the shell, but keep the nut meat intact.

Cheese Knife

The knife blade is used to cut a portion of cheese from the block/wedge/round and the forked point is used to pick up the portion and place it on individual plates.

You must provide separate knives for each cheese on the cheese board. Most cheeses have distinctive flavors. If the same knife is used on different cheeses it will cross-contaminate the flavors.

Cake Fork

The outside prongs of the cake fork are wider. It acts as a cutting edge to slice mouth-sized portions from the cake. A cake fork can be used instead of a dessert spoon and fork, ideal for cheesecake, gateau and meringue.

Parfait Spoon

A modern parfait is a dessert made of layers of fruit and ice cream (or yogurt or mousse) and served in a tall parfait glass. Because the glass is tall, a tall spoon is required to eat all the way to the bottom.

Polishing Cutlery Before Service

Dishwashers generally carry out a thorough cleaning process, but sometimes streaks remain on the cutlery. These need to be polished off by hand.

To do this, dip the cutlery into a bowl or jug of hot water containing a few drops of methylated spirits. Using a clean polishing cloth polish the hot cutlery and put onto a tray or straight into the drawer.

NOTE: Be careful not to handle the cutlery after cleaning. This ruins all the good work and can leave unsightly finger marks!

2. Hollow-ware

Traditionally, hollow-ware referred to silver service dishes and accessories, such as soup tureens, service bowls, sauceboats, cream jugs, sugar bowls, water pitchers, coffee pots and vases.

Today, many of these items are crockery and because they are a large feature of table setting they must blend with the general table design. However, always keep in mind all food items are best presented on a white background. When trying to enhance the color of food, do not confuse the colors by placing it on a highly patterned plate.

Types of Crockery

Type	Description
Bone China	It is very fine, hard crockery that is expensive to purchase. Metalized bone china has been developed as more robust crockery for regular use.
Vitrified (or Vitreous) Earthenware	This is a commercial grade earthenware, ideal if you do a lot of entertaining. It is generally more expensive but more durable than domestic earthenware.
Stoneware	This is a natural ceramic material which is fired at a very high temperature. It is very durable with high heat and shock resistance. Stoneware is usually more expensive than earthenware.
Porcelain	It is very hardy, having a semi-translucent appearance with a high resistance to chipping.

Bone China

Earthenware

Porcelain

Table Crockery

Plates

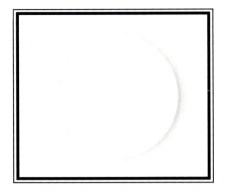 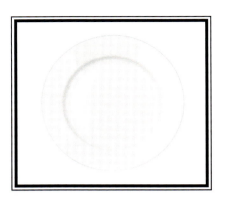 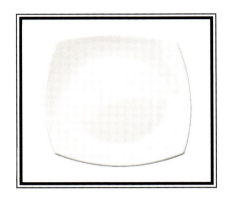

Side	Entree	Main
15 cm diameter	18 cm diameter	25 cm diameter
Used for bread. Set to left of forks. Also used as a cake plate.	Used for entree course, salads, cheese, or fruit.	Used for main meal. Often called a joint plate.
Used as an underplate for small bowls and cocktail dishes.	Used as an underplate for soup bowls or side salad bowls.	

Platters

Platters are large plates of any shape: round, oval, oblong, or according to the food (ex. a fish platter may be the shape of a fish). They are usually made of stoneware or stainless steel.

Coffee Cup and Saucer

Coffee cups and saucers come in two different sizes:

- A standard cup and saucer
- A small cup and saucer (demi-tasse)

Expensive espresso cups are insulated to retain the heat.

Tea Cup and Saucer

Tea cups are generally slighter smaller than coffee cups. Saucers for tea cups should be large enough to place the cup and a teaspoon alongside the cup. The teaspoon should be placed across the back of the cup, with the handle facing the same direction as the handle of the cup.

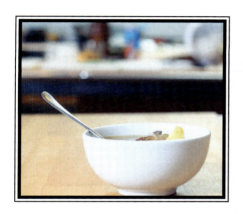

Cereal/Dessert Bowl

The standard cereal/dessert bowl is 13 cm in diameter. The traditional shape is deeper than a soup bowl to retain the heat of the food for as long as possible.

Soup

The standard soup bowl is 20 cm in diameter. A wide bowl allows space for an attractive soup garnish.

It is used to serve all types of soups, except consommé, which is traditionally served in a soup cup.

Pasta Bowl

Pasta is usually served with some kind of sauce. Because of the stickiness and oil content, pasta is best served in a bowl rather than on a flat plate. The bowl is wide, maybe up to 30 cm diameter.

Additional Crockery Items

Tea and Coffee Pots

Two main differences are:

1. The teapot is squat and round, whereas the coffee pot is taller and more oval shaped.
2. The teapot has a larger spout than the coffee pot.

Tea and coffee pots are usually made of:

- Stoneware
- China
- Silver or stainless steel

Tea Pot
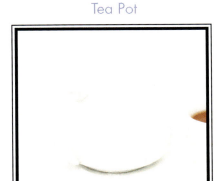

Coffee Pot
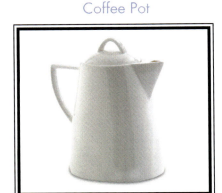

Milk and Cream Jugs

Milk Jug

Cream Jug
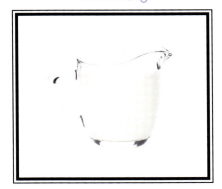

Milk and cream jugs are used to present milk/cream at the table. The cream jug is slightly smaller than the milk jug. Both should have a non-drip spout and a handle that is easy to hold.

Condiments (Cruet Set)

These are service receptacles for salt, ground pepper and mustard. Sometimes vinegar bottles and oil dishes are also added.

Salt shakers usually have less holes than pepper shakers. Instead of using ground pepper, some hostesses prefer to offer a pepper grinder. Condiments are usually offered for all savory food items.

Butter Dishes

Butter dishes are used to display individual butter portions on the table. They are usually smaller than a coffee saucer and should be accompanied by a butter knife.

Sauce Boat

A sauce boat is used to present a sauce to the table and is accompanied by an underplate and sauce ladle. It is also used to serve whipped cream at the table.

Traditionally, they were ornate and made of fine china. More modern ones are stainless steel.

Sugar Bowl

Sugar bowls are used to present sugar on the table or accompany tea/coffee service.

Where the sugar bowl is used with sugar cubes, it should always be accompanied by sugar tongs.

They should match the milk/cream jug if used as a set.

Oil Dishes

Oil dishes are shallow dishes filled with flavored oils to serve with dipping bread or salads. Oil and balsamic vinegar is served with some Italian food. These dishes can also be used for dipping sauces with rice paper wraps, or to serve chutney.

Glassware

Glassware used for Wine

White wine is traditionally served in tulip-shaped glassware and red wine in goblets. White wine glasses are generally smaller than red wine glasses. They may also have smaller rims. Sparkling wine glasses are tall and tulip-shaped. Some people, however, will serve sparkling wine in saucer-shaped glasses. Unfortunately, these allow the bubbles to "fizz out" which is not the desired effect.

Port glasses are small delicate glasses. Port is a fortified wine, high in alcohol, therefore smaller quantities are served. Wine glasses should be made of clear (and not colored) glass, to best see the color of the wine. Wine color is an indicator of a good wine or the correct wine.

Reasons for the Shape of Wine Glasses

White Wine Glass

Narrowness of the bowl allows white wine to retain its chilled temperature better than a wide bowl.

Red Wine Glass

A wider, rounder bowl gives red wine space to "breathe" and trap the characteristic aromas.

Sparkling Champagne Glass

The tall, narrow bowl reduces the area for handling the glass. Also less bubbles are lost with a small surface area. Part of the pleasure of drinking champagne is the "bubble feel" on the tongue, so don't forget it is not good to warm champagne!

PORT

Port is richer, sweeter and higher in alcohol than table wines, therefore small glasses are used. The aromas are best trapped by a narrow rim.

Glassware used for Spirits

MARTINI GLASS

Designed especially to serve a martini, a gin-based cocktail, it has fluted sides that slope out and come to a "V" in the center. The "V" is ideal for the placement of the olive.

BRANDY BALLOON

It has a short stem to "cup" the brandy to warm it in both hands. The narrow mouth traps the aroma of the warmed brandy.

HIGH BALL

This is a tall straight-sided glass used for drinks with lots of ice or liquid in them, such as a large rum and coke. It is heavy in the base and made of thick glass to keep the drink as chilled as possible.

TUMBLER

This is a short glass that is specially designed to stack. It is used for iced water or spirits on–the-rocks (with no mixer). It is easy to clear and ideal for buffets and large functions.

SHOT GLASS

This small glass is designed to hold a shot of whiskey. Over time it has been adapted to be used for other spirits or liqueurs. In some establishments shot glasses are used as nip measures.

LIQUEUR GLASS

These small "curvy" glasses are made to look elegant. It is designed to look full with one nip and to make it easy to drink the sweet (often very sticky) liquid. Most liqueur glasses have a short stem to lift the drink away from the table.

COCKTAIL GLASS

Cocktail glasses are designed to sell cocktails. Their curvy shapes and larger bowls allow for creative presentation of a cocktail and give plenty of room to add garnishes. Most glasses are suited to a single drink but some of the larger cocktail glasses are designed to share with many straws. Two common cocktails are Piña Colada and Margarita.

Glassware used for Beer

Beer glasses come in a variety of sizes and shapes. The common ones are as follows:

Pilsner

Nonic

Dimple

Tulip

Sleeve

Goblet

The most common sizes for a beer glass are:

- 200 ml
- 330 ml
- Pint (570 ml)

NOTES:

1. Some of the glass sizes are very close and should not be confused.
2. There will be variations in glass shapes according to modern and traditional designs.
3. Pints and half-pints may be referred to as "handles."
4. Different styles of glassware are chosen according to:
    a. The type of beer served
    b. The quantity of beer required
    c. The occasion
    d. Personal preference

Beer should always be served in chilled glasses.

Glassware used for Liqueur Coffee

A liqueur coffee is made of hot coffee, liqueur and sugar, then topped with a layer of thick cream.

The glass must be able to withstand heat and care is needed to pre-heat the glass when making liqueur coffee. The base of the glass must be heavy enough to prevent tipping.

The glassware used for serving liqueur coffee will be either:

A. Shielded by using serviette collars to hold the hot glass.
B. Specially designed for hot beverages, featuring toughened glass and a handle.

The Paris goblet glass is traditionally used for serving liqueur coffee, but the most common specially designed hot beverage glass is the Irish coffee glass.

Glassware used for Water and Fruit Juice

Glassware for water or fruit juice is either a variation of the tumbler or high ball. The glasses are usually straight sided to hold a large proportion of ice, and for ease of handling and storage.

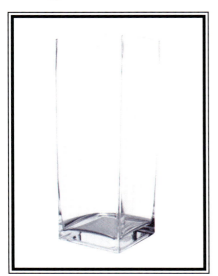

Chapter 3 Assignment

How many of these can you identify? Visit the online Resource Library to download this worksheet.

Chapter 4: Table Setting & Etiquette

- Table Setting
- Lay the Table Linen
- Add the Centerpiece
- Place the Cutlery
- Place the Glassware
- Add the Cruet Set, and any Accessories
- Finally, the Chairs
- Stand Back and Admire the Smart Presentation
- Table Etiquette
- Chapter 4 Assignment

TABLE SETTING

Table setting for a special occasion is not about just covering the table and setting down the cutlery. The dining table is the place where your guests will spend many hours eating the meal you have carefully planned, so the table deserves as much respect as the food.

Aim to create the most terrific table top you can. It begins with careful preparation of the dining area including cleaning the table and chairs (including the legs). Make sure the table linen is free of unwanted creases. All of the glassware and cutlery need to be cleaned and polished. Salt and pepper shakers must be filled, and all service equipment checked and kept handy on a sideboard. Your centerpiece ought to be prepared away from the table, but should be the first item to be place on the table after the cloth is laid correctly.

LAY THE TABLE LINEN

To ensure the cloth is correctly laid, check the following:

- The cloth is the correct side up.
- The drop on all sides is even.
- Corners are mitered (where required) to make all corners look tidy.

Placemats

Placemats are used in place of (or as well as) tablecloths, depending on the menu and style of service being offered. Tables with attractive wood, fiberglass or marble tops can be enhanced with color-coordinated placemats.

When placed on a table they should sit along the edge of the table and directly opposite the setting on the other side of the table.

Napkins

Napkins come in many different colors. These are used for the guests to wipe their hands on and can be folded in many different ways to enhance or complement the table setting.

Napkins are either placed in the center of every place setting (as a feature) or where they best suit the table design. The napkins should be approximately 50mm from the edge of the table and each one must be directly opposite the place setting on the other side of the table.

Some people want to make the napkin fold the feature of the table. There are various options, but remember they take time and are destroyed in seconds.

Add the Centerpiece

There is a huge range of options here, but a few basic principles need to be followed:

- Make sure the centerpiece (or pieces) matches the color theme of your table.
- Keep the centerpiece in proportion with the size of the table (not too big and overpowering).
- If choosing flowers, fresh is best.
- Do not choose flowers that are strongly scented.
- Beware of aphids, ants, or other bugs that may have hitchhiked on the flowers as they are not a good look on any dining table.
- There are no rules. You can choose candles, a sculpture, flags, paper craft, fruit bowl, or anything that fits with your theme or occasion.

Place the Cutlery

The first items to be set are the main knife and fork. Make sure these are placed wide enough so the main plate can be positioned easily between them. NOTE: a main plate is around 250mm wide, so the distance between the main knife and fork should be at least 280mm.

Remember:

- The blades of all knives should face to the left of the cover.
- The base of all cutlery should follow the "thumbnail rule."
- Cutlery should be set in a thumbnail from the edge of the table so it is all exactly in line. This will be approximately 15mm (See diagram at right).
- Outside the main knife place the entrée knife (blade facing left and in line a thumbnail from the edge of the table).
- Outside the main fork, place the entrée fork, using the thumbnail rule.
- Outside the entrée knife place the soup spoon.
- Tables look neat when the cutlery is laid on the table in a uniform way.
- At the head of the place setting the dessert spoon is set above the dessert fork, both facing the correct direction for use.
- The side knife (on side plate) should be in line with rest of cutlery to the left of the cover. NOTE: the side knife should be 1/3 from the right of the side plate to allow space for a bread roll to be served.

Place the Glassware

Place the wine glass directly above the main knife, approximately 15mm from the tip of the blade.

If serving more than one wine, place each of the additional wine glasses diagonally to the left of the first wine glass to be used.

NOTE: Hold each glass up to the light to check for cleanliness before placement.

If water glasses are part of the table setting, they are usually set to the right of the wine glasses.

The diagram to the right shows a classical table setting, set for serving three different wines and a four course meal, such as a soup, entrée, main course and dessert.

Sell your books at sellbackyourBook.com!
Go to sellbackyourBook.com and get an instant price quote. We even pay the shipping - see what your old books are worth today!

Inspected By: Johan_Corredor

0007906334 1

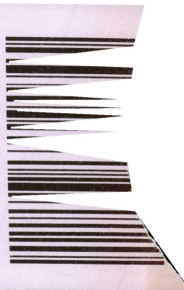

Add the Cruet Set and any Accessories (such as place names or party favors)

Check that the cruets (salt and pepper) are full and give them a last-minute polish before placing them together on the center of the table. One cruet set should be provided for 4-6 guests. For larger numbers, several cruet sets should be available.

For a smart and uniform look to the table, make sure place names and accessories are in the identical place at each setting. Do not clutter the table.

Finally, the Chairs!

Now the table is set, place each chair adjacent to each cover, exactly central and exactly opposite each other.

The chairs should just kiss the table cloth.

Dina Says:
Attention to detail gives an event an overall sense of cohesiveness. People may not know exactly what it is that keeps their eyes flowing, but they will definitely feel it.

Stand Back and Admire the Smart Presentation

TABLE ETIQUETTE

The definition of "etiquette" is best described as a "code of polite behavior" or "being socially acceptable." When considering table etiquette there are a number of "correct procedures" established as appropriate behavior:

1. The meal will begin when the host or hostess unfolds his or her napkin. It is the guests' signal to do the same.//
2. When opening the napkin, it is appropriate to unfold it rather than shake it open before placing it on the lap.
3. Always dab your mouth clean with the napkin, rather than wipe it. Never use it to wipe your nose!
4. Do not adjust the cutlery, play with the cutlery setting, or polish the cutlery with your napkin while waiting for the food to arrive.
5. Do not start to eat until the host or hostess begins eating.
6. Using your table setting, start with the utensils (cutlery) farthest from your plate for the first course, and work your way in for the following courses.
7. Never eat off your knife, or with your fingers when utensils are available.
8. Once your cutlery has been used for eating a course, do not return them to the table. To signal you have completed the course, place your knife and fork together with the handles facing the base of the place and the blade and prongs facing the top of the plate.
9. Do not stretch across the table, crossing other guests, to reach for condiments or food items.
10. If another guest asks you to pass them something while you are eating, put your cutlery down on your plate before assisting.
11. Always use the serving utensils to help yourself to food, not your own eating utensils.
12. Do not talk with food in your mouth.
13. Taste your food before adding seasoning.
14. When eating soup, or a liquid or semi-liquid food, always scoop the spoon serving away from you.
15. Never blow on your food to cool it down.
16. Portion a reasonable mouthful size of food at a time. Do not stuff your mouth so full to cause a danger of it spilling back out.
17. It is acceptable to leave some food on your plate when you have eaten enough. If the food is not to your liking it is polite to attempt to eat a small amount of it.

18. Try and pace your eating so that you are not seen as a "gulp master" or as the one that everyone is getting tired of waiting for.
19. Keep your elbows off the table.
20. Do not dominate the conversation or remain obviously silent. Make an effort to share the conversation around and involve the quiet ones.
21. Never eat loudly, slurp or burp.
22. Never push your plate away when you have finished with it, or stack your own plate with other guests' plates in an effort to clear place settings.
23. When drinking wine, hold your glass by the stem, not the bowl.
24. Never have your cell phone on during a dinner party. If you are expecting an emergency situation, inform your host or hostess and apologize for any inconvenience in advance.
25. Never groom yourself at the table, such as run a quick comb through your hair, apply lipstick, or use dental floss.

Chapter 4 Assignment

Spot the Faults

The place setting below contains faults according to the establishment requirements. Spot the faults and jot them down in the space provided below. Visit the online Resource Library to download this worksheet.

Chapter 5: Project Dinner Party

- Project Content
- Project Design
- Dinner Party Time
- Create the Menu
- Wine and Drink Guide
- Chapter 5 Assignment

PROJECT CONTENT

Notes	Content	Activities
Introduction	Project design How to create a mood board The Dinner Party	
Create the vision	Decide on the style of your party Determine your budget Choose your theme and color Decide on the dress code Determine who will host the party Decide on the format of the occasion Draw up your guest list	1. Create your Dinner Party vision 2. Begin collecting images for your mood board
Case study describing the vision of a dinner party		
Plan the concept	The A8 recipe of planning and design: 1. Attire 2. Accessories 3. Anticipation 4. Arrival 5. Atmosphere 6. Appetite 7. Amusement 8. Appreciation	Own notes on each of the ingredients of the A8 recipe 3. Design and plan your Dinner party 4. Final concepts and details represented on your mood board
Case study of the party planning and design details		
DIY Dinner party checklist	2-3 weeks before A week before The day of the party Immediately after	

PROJECT DESIGN

This module is designed to work through both stages of planning a dinner party:

1. Create the vision, and
2. Develop the concept

Each stage will be explained then a case study will be provided to illustrate the details. As you progress through the project you will be encouraged to jot down your own ideas on the worksheet templates provided in the Resource Library and develop a mood board of your dinner party style and design.

How to create a Mood Board

Express your inspirations by creating a collage of your favorite theme photos, colors and styles. Follow these steps:

For a digital mood board:

1. Browse online galleries and your own photos.
2. Drag, drop, resize and position your images onto the board, adding text if you like.
3. Share your design by posting your profile page for others to comment on like Pinterest, Instagram, or Facebook.

For a non-digital mood board (your own homemade poster):

1. Gather all the images you have taken photos of, cut out of magazines or printed from websites such as Pinterest, Tumblr, or Flickr.
2. Place the image that inspires you the most in a prominent position on your board.
3. Arrange the other images and extend your story around your main inspiration point.
4. Keep it simple and let it flow.

Dinner Party Time

Whenever there is mention of a dinner party, images start forming of a stunning dinner table, scrumptious food, an inviting space for guests and a perfect music playlist. Ultimately, that is what you should be aiming for whether the occasion is somewhat exoti or a simple three-course affair. Let your inspiration come from what you love to do. Your dinner party should be an extension of your personality.

A dinner party is given for a variety of reasons. It may celebrate a grand occasion or it might be just an excuse to get together with friends. It is a way of celebrating life with style. The perfect home dinner party is best with six or eight people, where the food will be served at the table, conversation includes everyone, and people don't split into their own immediate talking groups. For numbers of guests larger than twelve, change the style of service to a buffet or cocktail party.

If holding an adult only party, please make the adorable family dog absent for the occasion, exclude the cat, and see if you can hire a babysitter or give them their own party by suggesting a sleepover at Grandma's house.

One of the biggest debates around modern dinner party etiquette is the seating arrangements. The old-fashioned attention to seating arrangements has considerable merit. It requires the host and hostess to sit at opposite ends of the table; couples never sit together; and males and females are alternated around the table. It allows the host and hostess to attend to their guests' needs at each end of the table and divides the conversation evenly. In today's social environment, such restrictions are considered too steeped in formality. Many hosts prefer to seat their guests to complement different personalities. It may be a disaster, for example, to sit two highly opinionated people together.

Another modern trend is for guests to bring a bottle of wine to share at the dinner party. This is a lovely gesture, but can sometimes interfere with the wine and food pairing you have prepared. If this is the case, thank your guest and tell him/her you will be sure to enjoy it on another occasion. On the other hand, if you have not matched wine with the food, then go ahead and grab a bottle opener to share the delicious wine with the rest of your guests.

Even at the most formal dinner party, do not compromise timely service of lovely hot food for dining etiquette. It is not worth sticking to the old-fashioned rules of refraining from starting to eat before the host starts, especially if the host is busy serving wine and every one's dinner is getting cold.

There is a difference between traditional etiquette and good manners. The host and hostess will reflect good manners, but so should all the guests. Simple examples are helping others to be seated, offering others food before serving yourself, and not dominating the dining space by propping yourself up on your elbows while eating (just to name a few).

CREATE THE MENU

Creating a dinner party menu takes more skill than you think to get it right. The key is simplicity. A common mistake is to try and do too much. Here is a "toolbox" of good instructions that will help you enjoy the process and create a wonderful taste balance.

1. Gather up your cookbooks, pour a glass of your favorite wine, grab a pen and paper and settle into your best planning mode.

2. Note the dietary restrictions you know some of your guests might have. This doesn't mean you have to cook a separate meal for this person, but you might like to make a special effort to avoid certain foods, or create choices to satisfy the food preferences of everyone.

3. Vegetarianism deserves a special point all on its own. It is bad manners for the vegetarian to announce their food preference at the time of serving. Also it is bad manners for another guest at the table to say "oh, you are a vegetarian" when they see someone choosing from the side dishes only. Because many people decide to reduce their meat intake, cater for the vegetarians on your guest list by having liberal servings of vegetables as side dishes. Do not use meaty bits, like bacon, to garnish the vegetable dishes.

4. Think about the ingredients that are in season. Nothing beats "fresh" when it comes to food.

5. Choose the dishes for each course beginning with what you really want to make and then plan the rest of the menu around this feature item.

6. Don't choose recipes that all need cooking at the last minute to make you flustered just before serving time. A well-known restaurant trick is to choose braises because you can marinate or even cook them the day before. This allows flavors to permeate through the meat making it taste better.

7. Check that you have been kind to digestion by choosing a lighter dessert with a rich main course, or vice versa. A menu with three very rich courses might lead to stomach complaints or sleepiness for your guests.

8. When you have prepared your menu test it for balance of color, texture, flavor, ingredients, and cooking methods.

9. If you are serving a different wine for each course, match the wine type with the dominant flavors. If you plan on serving one wine throughout the meal, make your best choice according to the flavor combinations you have chosen.

10. Write your shopping list, taking care to allow a little flexibility with some of the ingredients, especially those that might look better on the day you go shopping.

Menu suggestions

The following menus are based on three courses that could be either pre-plated or served family-style on platters at the table. The best thing about pre-plating food is you can control the presentation. The best thing about platters is the food looks more generous. The style of service brings out the communal spirit in all the guests as they share the food and pass the platters to each other.

Never think dinner parties require unlimited financial resources to make them memorable and enjoyable. It is easy to go to the food market and spend lots of money on expensive ingredients, but it is not necessary. With some clever kitchen skills you can make delicious meals out of less expensive cuts of meat and fabulous side dishes out of in-season vegetables.

1. Starter suggestions

Credit crunch	Middle-of-the-road	Dream budget
French onion soup	Road butternut soup with avocado	Calamari with mushrooms, olives and rocket
Curried asparagus soup	Chicken, grape and almond salad	Guinness and blue stilton soup
Chicken liver pate	Whiskey smoked salmon quiche	Spinach and ricotta gnocchi
Portobello mushrooms stuffed with leek and parmesan	Veal and apricot terrine	King prawns poached in lemon butter with watercress pesto
Chermoula-spiced chicken and mushroom kebabs	Enchilada tuna melts	Smoked venison carpaccio with walnut salsa
Roast pumpkin and parmesan orzo with feta	Crabmeat ravioli with browned butter and snowpeas	Goat's cheese souffle with glazed baby beetroot and orange segments

2. Main course suggestions

Credit crunch	Middle-of-the-road	Dream budget
Osso bucco	Chicken napoletata	Beef wellington
Coq au vin	Prawn and green mango curry	Salmon in prosciutto with lime and sweet chili dressing
Beef and guinness casserole	Rack of lamb with red wine and rosemary jus	Glazed crispy duck with ginger and hazelnut jus
Meatballs in spicy tomato sauce	Beef schnitzel filled with ham and parmesan cheese	Eye fillet mignon with syrah demi-glace
Smoked chicken and cranberry frittata	Pork fillet with tangy plum sauce	Lobster newburg
Spaghetti carbonara with mushrooms and bacon	Veal paprika with sour cream	Maple-garlic marinated pork tenderloin
Lentil patties on wholemeal bruschetta	Lamb cassoulet	Moroccan lamb with shiraz honey sauce
	Beef bourguignon	

3. Dessert suggestions

Credit crunch	Middle-of-the-road	Dream budget
Crême brulée	Fresh berry bavarois	Bitter chocolate tart with blackberry compote and vanilla cream
Five spice panna cotta with dried fruit compote	Chocolate, date and almond torte	White chocolate and mascarpone mousse with pineapple braised in orange liqueur
Chocolate sponge roll filled with cream and berries	Individual lemon delicious	Amaretto cheesecake with strawberries
Apple and berry pancakes	Chocolate brownie with hot fudge topping	Siennese panforte
Rhubarb and berry crumble	Apricot, almond and vanilla tarte tartin	Tiramisu cake
Orange and cinnamon jelly with macerated orange slices	Roast winter fruits with butterscotch yogurt	Orange, cardamom and grand marnier sponge

4. Three course dinner party menus

Credit crunch three course dinner party menu:

Course	Title of dish	Description
Starter	Carrot, orange and cranberry salad	Carrots grated or cut in julienne strips, with diced orange and dried cranberries, mixed with orange vinaigrette, served in a lettuce cup and garnished with parsley
Main	Braised beef with red wine sauce	Braised beef in sauce made from beef stock, onions, mushrooms and bacon flavored with thyme
Vegetables	Buttered baby potatoes with green beans and toasted almonds Grilled tomatoes filled with garlic and parmesan breadcrumbs	
Dessert	Cheese crusted apple pie and whipped cream	A light cheese pastry base with an apple cinnamon and lemon filling topped with pecan nut and brown sugar crumble

Middle-of-the-road three course dinner party menu:

Course	Title of dish	Description
Starter	Avocado tomato and mozzarella salad	Sliced avocado, tomato and mozzarella with fresh basil and topped with balsamic vinaigrette
Main	Chicken fillets with apricot ginger sauce	Chicken breasts with sauce made from apricot nectar, grated fresh ginger, soya sauce and sliced green shallots, garnished with fresh rocket leaves
Vegetables	Crispy sweet and sour rice with red pepper and pineapple Snow peas in garlic mint butter Carrot sticks	
Dessert	Coffee ice cream with chocolate brandy sauce	Homemade ice cream and chocolate brandy sauce alternated in a stemmed parfait glass, and garnished with a single large strawberry

Dream budget three course dinner party menu:

Course	Title of dish	Description
Starter	Seafood tartlets with lemon saffron sauce	Scallops, squid and king prawns in a lemon cream sauce served in a light crisp pastry shell
Main	Seasoned pheasant with prunes and port	Boned out pheasant with veal, ham, pinenut, prune and port stuffing, cooked in a vegetable flavored stock
Vegetables	Pan fried potatoes with bacon and chopped shallots Asparagus spears with hollandaise sauce Roasted red pepper slices	
Dessert	Marinated strawberries with mango sorbet	Slice strawberries marinated in a strawberry liqueur serves with mango sorbet and garnished with a spring of mint

There should be no difference in the "delicious factor" between a dream budget dinner party menu and a credit-crunch budget menu. The main differences lie in:

- The cost of the ingredients
- The complexity of preparation
- The style of pre-dinner drinks and wines served
- The quality of the tableware and glassware

You certainly don't have to wait for the best imported caviar or serve a multi-course French traditional menu to reach "dream budget" status. You could, however, offer a few more courses, therefore the serving sizes for each course would become smaller. One course that adds an exotic touch to a dinner menu is a sorbet, designed to refresh the palate between the starter and the main course.

Examples of sorbets are:

- Pinot Gris sorbet and soaked melon
- Apple and Calvados sorbet
- Lime sorbet
- Basil Mint sorbet
- Champagne sorbet
- Watermelon sorbet
- Zesty Lemon sorbet

Wine and Drink Guide

Once you have decided on your menu you need to think about drinks. It is better to have an oversupply of drinks for the dinner party, rather than run out midway through the meal. If supplies are limited, however, you can slow the top-ups by serving the dessert course a little earlier than scheduled. The following guidelines might help:

- It is good to greet your guests with something bubbly or stimulating as a pre-dinner drink. This could be champagne, sparkling mineral water, soda water or lager. For more up-market dinner parties venture into the realm of cocktails. Allow 2 glasses per person. You will get 6 glasses from one bottle of champagne.

- Have a ready supply of iced water (flavored with lemon, cucumber or mint if you prefer) on hand as required.

- Allow half a bottle of wine per person when calculating quantities to have with dinner. Each bottle should be 6 servings.

- Consider a glass each of late-harvest sweet wine with dessert. The bottles are small and you should allow 6-8 servings per bottle.

- If the budget allows, have a small selection of liqueurs available to serve with coffee, or offer specialty coffees if you are an expert barista.

Chapter 5 Assignment

Create a dinner party menu, including food and wine pairing for low, medium, and high budgets. Visit the online Resource Library to download this worksheet.

Course	Credit-crunch	Middle-of-the-road	Dream budget
Starter			
Main			
Vegetables			
Dessert			

Chapter 6: Dinner Party Planning

- Dinner Party Planning
- Dinner Party Vision
- Mood Board Ideas
- Hostess Tips
- Plan the Concept
- Madison's Dinner Party Planning and Design Details
- Design and Plan Your Dinner Party
- Chapter 6: Final Project

Dinner Party Planning

To get started on planning your dinner party, you'll need to follow these three important steps:

1. Create the vision where you generate the "look, feel and outcome."
2. Develop the concept before handing it over to others who can assist.
3. Enjoy all the credit for a fun and memorable event.

Create the Vision

Search for as many ideas as possible to plan the best dinner party. Look on the Internet, thumb through magazines, talk with people who have graduated in previous years about what "works" for a party. Make lists, create a folder or file to keep all your photos, clippings, fabulous hints and suggestions from other people, phone numbers and scribbled notes together.

Decide on the Style of the Dinner Party

For this study program we will focus on indoor dinner parties served at the table at a private residence. Of course you can host a dinner party in a function room as a banquet or for larger numbers with buffet service, but these will be topics of other programs. When considering the style of your dinner party, choose the best service style that would suit your menu. Will you pre-plate all the food in the kitchen or have your guests serve themselves from platters on the table? You may even include a combination of pre-plating the meat portion and serving the vegetables at the table?

Determine your budget

You can entertain on any sized budget. Never be put off because your disposable income is not as great as you would like it to be. Never think you have to impress your guests by choosing high-end ingredients. Cost out your chosen menu and if it is higher than your budget allows, substitute the higher cost items with something a little more economical.

Choose your dinner party theme

Build your dinner party theme around the food. This might be a type of cuisine (Indian, Spanish, Italian, Vietnamese), or a season (Summer Seafood, Fall Fantasies, Winter Warmers or Spring Specials), or an ingredient (pumpkin, zucchini, cherry or orange). The last suggestion goes against all menu planning principles, but could be fun.

Decide on dress code

Don't impose a dress code unless you are wishing to highlight a special theme of your dinner party, such as "wear your best saris and shalwar kameez for our Indian feast", or "arrive in something depicting our new season." Trust your friends will know the effort you will go to over the food and make equal effort with their appearance.

Determine who will host the party

This is your dinner party, so you will host it. If you are in a partnership, share the hosting role and the preparation. It is more fun to do all the cleaning, polishing, setting, chopping, stirring, blending and baking together. Decide where your individual strengths lie and share the tasks accordingly.

Decide on the date, time and format of the occasion

Remember a dinner party will be reasonably formal and will feature more than you would normally eat or drink at a family meal, so it is best to host it on a day when your guests do not have an early start the next morning. Friday and Saturday nights are good times to host dinner parties for working people. There are many fashions and individual preferences about the time of dining. Some hosts prefer to begin eating around 7:00 - 7:30pm and dine at a leisurely pace allowing for good digestion and stimulating conversation. Other hosts like to relax with their guests first and dine around 9:00pm. Be very careful about early drinking and late dining. The food you have carefully chosen should not be viewed through hazy inebriated eyes.

Allow around 45-60 minutes for pre-dinner drinks, so if you invite your guests for 7:00pm you should plan to start the meal around 8:00pm. Presuming conversation reigns throughout the evening the usual format for a dinner party is:

- Welcome and pre-dinner drink service
- Seat your guests for the meal
- Begin with the first course(s) and matching wines
- Serve the main course and change the wine glasses if a different wine is served
- Serve dessert
- Serve coffee at the dining table or in a more relaxed setting in the lounge
- Bid everyone farewell

Draw up the guest list

Generally we consider the guests most important to the occasion and choose the number to suit the dining space. We all ponder over personalities and prefer to invite those who we think will be compatible. Consider including an extra surprise guest, someone no-one else knows. They might be a single person among couples or someone new to town. For everyone who shudders at the risk others will consider it truly hospitable.

Unless the dinner party is very formal, use the phone, invite your guests face-to-face, or send an email. A savvy hostess will take this opportunity to inquire about any particular food preferences.

Dinner Party Vision

Madison's Dream Budget Dinner Party

Madison is in her early 40's, single and a high-flying business executive in a large corporation. She has a high disposable income and loves to entertain. Madison developed an early love for cooking when her parents owned a 4-star hotel. She used to help the chef in the kitchen during her college holidays.

Madison gets spring fever every year. Like a butterfly emerging from a winter chrysalis she gives her condominium a makeover, renews a few furnishings and refreshes all of her surroundings. Many of her work engagements have required overseas travel over the last few months so she is looking forward to staying at home for a while and catching up with a few friends over dinner. She decided to invite six of her closest friends and Keaton, a man she has dated on occasions in between her overseas trips. None of her friends knew Keaton but were keen to become acquainted.

The vision of the dinner party was as follows:

A. A semi-formal dinner party
B. Dream budget
C. Theme: Champagne, Crayfish and Cabaret music
D. Dress to impress
E. Hosted by Madison
F. Saturday 25 May, 7:00pm. Pre-dinner drinks. Dinner served at 8:30pm
G. 8 guests (friends) invited by personalized invitations

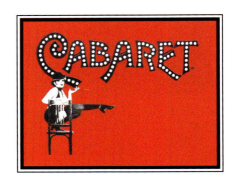

MOOD BOARD IDEAS

ACTIVITY 1: CREATE THE DINNER PARTY VISION

Your dinner party "vision" worksheet
Style
Budget
Theme and color
Dress code
Hosting notes
Date, time and format
Guest list

ACTIVITY 2: BEGIN DESIGNING YOUR MOOD BOARD

Collect images of your dinner party vision and paste them together in a mood board of your own. Visit the online Resource Library to download this worksheet.

Hostess Tips

The hostess's role begins with the first attempt at the menu design right through to when you can consider putting your feet up for the first time after the dinner party is over. It is not all about floating around the guests, smiling, looking glamorous and having fun. This is usually a clever disguise while checking all preparations are on cue, all mishaps are dealt with without anyone knowing, everyone has enough food and drink, all preparations are working to plan, and no-one is left without conversation or participation.

Don't be too formal and stuffy in front of your guests. Go for elegance, not fussiness.

Here are some tips to help you achieve the status of "super-hostess:"

Learn the art of conversation

A dinner party is really easy if the conversation flows around you and all you hear is a background of chatter and laughter. For the quieter moments and times when the conversation needs refreshing you will need to be at your best. Be inclusive but never monopolize the chat with your own agenda.

Be a smart planner

Draw up a planning schedule in your diary. It is no use thumbing through your recipe books looking for ideas on the day before the party. Always serve something you know how to cook well. If a new recipe sounds exciting, test it out a week or two ahead and get it perfect for the night.

Consider hiring someone in the kitchen for behind scene preparation

If you are hosting the party alone (and if the budget allows) hire someone to keep an eye on last minute preparations and service while you are circulating around your guests. You need to ensure all your guests are comfortable with each other and you cannot oversee this if you are confined to the kitchen.

Develop an unshakable attitude

Before your guests arrive use the best method you know to relax and chill out. In the case of an entertainment crisis, handle it with grace and tact. If you think that might be advice your grandmother would give you, she's right. No use losing your cool because something became burnt, spilt or broken.

Equip the washroom

Make sure this room is as well-appointed as the dining area. Apart from being sparkling clean, make sure the soap is replenished in the pump bottle. Include a vase of flowers and light some candles. Do not expect one guest towel will be enough for the evening. Have a good supply of rolled up individual cloth napkins for hand drying.

Never dread the cleaning up

Start with a clean kitchen counter/bench and all the prepared foods refrigerated or waiting to be assembled or cooked. Clean as you go. Make full use of your dishwasher rather than stack the used dishes in your sink. Stay organized. After everyone has left, turn up your music, kick off your party shoes, and celebrate the night while attending to the last of the cleanup. Remember, it is best to attend to it that night rather than face the remains the next morning.

Dina Says:

It's all in the details... little bits of special make for one amazing experience.

Plan the Concept

Here we are going to "walk through" the A8 recipe of planning and design. Visit the online Resource Library to download this worksheet (attached to the Chapter 1 Assignment):

1. Attire
2. Accessories
3. Anticipation
4. Arrival
5. Atmosphere
6. Appetite
7. Amusement
8. Appreciation

1. Attire

Fashion experts would insist on dress codes to be established for all occasions. You need to decide whether this is truly necessary. The more formal the occasion the more you would like to ensure your guests will not turn up in denims, tennis shoes, and cotton tees. For these occasions it is best to save the embarrassment and make your recommendations.

Whether holding a credit-crunch dinner party or a dream budget soirée your guests should know the appropriate attire is "dressy casual." For women this means silk pants, dress pants, a skirt and semi-formal top, or dress. For men trousers and a collared shirt is appropriate. There should be no distinction in attire between host and guest.

2. Accessories

Good grooming and decorum are the best accessories. Dress leather or patent shoes and stylish well-chosen belts, dress jewelry, a toning scarf and pretty buckle or bow are all acceptable. A tie is optional for men.

Decorate your table according to the season unless you have decided on a color theme. Do not overdo the accessories. Never let the decorations detract from the visual appeal of the food. Use yellows, hibiscus and shells in the summer; colored leaves in Fall; rosehips and evergreen leaves in winter; and pastels, blossoming branches and daffodils in spring. Bring nature inside with flowers, leaves, berries, twigs and fruits, but make sure you leave the livestock (ants, spiders and beetles) outside.

3. Anticipation

Anticipation should build for your guests as soon as you invite them to your dinner party. If you have an established reputation as a great hostess your guests will already look forward to the next occasion. The way you communicate with them will determine the enthusiasm they will have for the occasion. By showing enthusiasm, being accommodating and receptive to individual needs helps build anticipation. In some ways we prefer to use themes and surprise activities to build anticipation. Hopefully whatever is unknown for the guest is going to create fascination.

Creating anticipation for your guests at the dinner party can mean the difference between an average meal and an exceptional one. You need to turn your guests from observers into participants. Instead of being passive recipients of whatever conversation comes their way, they should be active and inclusive.

Anticipation should continue throughout the entire dinner party, from pre-dinner drinks, at the beginning of every course, right up to coffee and beyond. You could provide everyone with a printed menu if you wish, but it is not necessary. Intrigue will gather from the thoughts "I wonder what she is going to serve next."

4. Arrival

Make sure you have a music playlist organized to begin before the doorbell rings and doesn't end until the last guest departs. A delicious food aroma wafting to the front door is often enough to say welcome. Acknowledge each guest's arrival with a genuine and assuring greeting. Tell them how honored you are to have them share the occasion with you.

People handle the task of "ice-breaking" differently. Some launch straight into formal introductions while others give a prompt for guests to introduce themselves. Many go in for ice-breaker games which can be fun for some, but a yawn for others. Another clever way of introducing and mixing people is to try not to have everything prepared in the kitchen before they arrive, so they can pitch in and help. If you think this goes against all hospitality etiquette, try it and see how guests like to gravitate to the kitchen.

5. Atmosphere

It is definitely time to dim the lights for dinner parties. A soft glow makes people feel glamorous. Avoid using scented candles that might interrupt with the delicious smell of food. If you have been bothered by fast melting wax candles, try refrigerating them before use and see how much slower they burn. Time to polish the silver candelabra for the high-end dinner party but you can also create an intimate atmosphere with small tea candles.

Dinner parties are not the occasions to raise the volume of rock, rap or heavy metal. By all means choose your favorite music, but keep the volume down so people can talk. Remember the food should take center stage, not the sound. Formal dinner parties lend themselves to light orchestral or sound tracks from movies or shows. Search out some café music titles such as Martin Winch's Espresso Guitar.

Decorate with flowers. A flower piece in the center of the table is delightful if small and toning with the table setting colors you have chosen. Remember to keep them low so guests on either side of the table can see each other.

6. Appetite

Dinner parties lend themselves to the service of signature cocktails. In winter, replace these with goblets of mulled wine. Not only will mulled wine warm your guests from the inside, but the spicy aroma will drift to the front door and create an instant welcome.

Snacks, like nuts, cheese straws or olives are not essential to start a dinner party. Be guided by how many pre-dinner drinks you wish to serve. If you decide on a "drink early and dine later" format then your host responsibility skills will guide you into serving snacks with drinks. Dress them up in silver or crystal bowls for a better look.

Have your dining table set before your guests arrive and always use a fabric table cloth. The use of cloth napkins for special occasions is essential; in fact try to use them on your table

settings at all dinner parties, except if you want to create a special fold in which case paper creases more precisely than cloth. No need to reinforce advice on having all your cutlery and glassware polished beforehand. Make sure each place setting is perfectly positioned.

If you have a seating plan, put place names at each place setting. First names are all you need. You could attach the names to a neatly presented party favor or have them displayed as a small flag or badge.

Whatever color you choose for the table cloth or table accents (like runners), do not choose colorful dinner plates that clash with the cloth. Let the food provide the color. White is best to show off the natural colors of food. Like the saying "you can never have too many black shoes in your wardrobe" you can also never have too many white plates in your kitchen cupboards.

When dinner is ready to be served, have the candles lit and water glasses filled. A simple "Dinner is ready. Would you like to be seated?" should be short and sweet enough to lead the way to the table. If the first course is cold, it is perfectly acceptable to have it already set on the table. Take care not to spoil your place settings though. If you have made a feature of the napkin, place name and party favor, allow your guests time to enjoy this before the food is served.

Keep with the old refinement of serving ladies before men if the food is plated. Place each plate from the guest's left side if possible. For family-style service let guests serve themselves from platters on the table. You might like to suggest a systematic movement of the platters around the table, or you could take the friendly approach of asking if you can serve others from the platter nearest you. Since this procedure can take time, suggestion should be made for those who already have their meal to make a start. Keep all food on the table warm in case guests require extra helpings.

Do not clear the plates from each course until all guests have finished. Where possible, clear the plates from the right of each person two at a time. Do not scrape or stack plates at the table. After the main course, remove all serving platters, side plates, condiments, bread baskets, butter, salt and pepper. The table should look completely clear of all items served with the main course before dessert is served. If you wish to delay dessert service to relax over conversation, don't have everyone looking at the aftermath of the main course while they are talking.

Throughout the night, don't forget to keep your guests hydrated. This does not mean ply them with alcohol. Make sure there is plenty of water on hand, iced water if possible. It is a good idea to fill several carafes of water and have them chilled in the refrigerator so you don't run out.

Switch the scenery for coffee if you can. This might not be a popular suggestion if a convivial atmosphere has already been created at the dining table. By moving to more comfortable seating in the lounge, your guests get a chance to begin new conversations and relax for the remainder of the evening. Make coffee service into a mini course all of its own. Offer alternatives such as tea, herb tea, or hot chocolate and serve with sweet morsels such as Turkish delight, candied ginger, nougat or homemade truffles. You may wish to offer a glass of port, brandy or liqueur as the final "nightcap." Never underestimate the power of your final offerings at a dinner party. A delicious ending accentuates the lasting memory.

7. Amusement

When planning a dinner party the goal is to help everyone to have a good time and to enjoy stimulating and free-flowing conversation over good food.

No one enjoys uncomfortable pauses in conversation or dialogue that is forced. If people are invited to a dinner party they should expect to be social and help stimulate conversation. A good conversationalist has a range of topics to choose from and doesn't stick to the stock standard questions about job, marital status, or family. Upcoming local events are safe topics. Plenty of people like to hear about scandalous, outrageous or debatable issues, but it is best to know your audience before launching into sensitive subject matter.

The food and conversation is entertaining in its own right, but if the conversation is wearing a little thin, or if you wish to slow down the alcohol consumption you might like to draw on an activity to provide a diversion. Some light-hearted suggestions include movie trivial pursuits or charades. Another old favorite is to have some "After 8" flat dinner mints. One by one each guest tilts their head back and has to get the dinner mint into their mouth by moving their head, but not using their hands.

The best dinner party game is "message under the plate." At the beginning of the meal everyone is to read the message you placed earlier under their plate, but is not allowed to share the contents with anyone. It might be a question to ask another guest, for example "have you ever eaten crickets?" or a strange statement like "I have often wondered what it would be like to be a bird." Sometime during the meal each guest must ask the question or use the phrase as naturally as they can in conversation. The person who is able to slip the message into conversation without anybody noticing is the winner. The person who is the last to use their allotted message is the loser!

8. Appreciation

It is good planning to create the party favors for a dinner party as an extension to the memorable meal. Give each guest something to take home to savor and reinforce your hostess qualities. Dinner party favors lend themselves to be something that could be nibbled on the way home (spiced almonds, ginger cookies, orange and cranberry shortcake), or enjoyed for breakfast the next morning (homemade granola or marmalade, or a special brand of herb tea). Choose food items that can be made and wrapped well in advance so the day of the party is free for food preparations. There is nothing wrong with making a double recipe of the sweets you prepared to have for coffee and providing gift packs of them to take home.

The success of a dinner party is shown by the appreciation of the guests. Good guest etiquette is to (a) phone or write and thank the host for the wonderful occasion, and (b) return the invitation by hosting a dinner party at a later date.

Madison's Dinner Party Planning & Design Details

Attire

As it was a spring evening and still a little cool, Madison wore a black silk dress. The female guests wore either dress trousers and shirts or an evening dress with jacket. The male guests wore dark dress trousers and open-neck dress shirts. Some wore jackets or waist coats and dress scarves which they were comfortable to remove when seated at the dining table.

Accessories

Being a traditionalist when it comes to food service, Madison believes in crisp white linen table cloths with minimum table decoration. She used slightly starched whole linen napkins, folded them as cabaret fans and placed them at the center of every place setting. Along the table she had three low crystal vases of red roses and pink tulips to symbolize happiness, confidence and caring with a subtle romantic blend. Rather than use place names Madison put a small printed note of welcome at the head of each place setting.

Clothing accessories worn by the guests were as impressive as their attire. Madison wore complimentary beaded earrings and necklace. The female guests took up the cabaret theme and wore long beads or beaded chokers, arm or wrist bracelets, and large ringed earrings. As all guests were corporate people the men wore designer watches and some wore expensive dress rings.

Shoes, belts and handbags were represented by Christian Louboutin, Manolo Blahnik, Gucci and Prada.

Anticipation

Madison spotted some stylish invitations so bought them three weeks before she decided to have the dinner party. Not all her friends knew she was back from overseas and rather than phone and get caught up in lengthy conversation, she wrote:

"I am anxious to celebrate spring, so please join me for a Champagne, Crayfish and Cabaret dinner party at my condo on Saturday, May 25th starting with pre-dinner drinks at 7:00pm. Dress to impress; besides there is someone I would like you to meet. Give me a call or text me ASAP."

Anticipation was generated as soon as Madison's friends knew she was back in the city. This was further triggered by their eagerness to be treated by her great choice of food once again and by the intriguing comment on the invitation "besides there is someone I would like you to meet." Mmmm, had this girl fallen in love at long last?

Arrival

Madison was her usual comfortable, relaxed, but gracious self when she opened the door to all her guests. A smile, embrace and kiss on both cheeks made everyone feel welcome and eager to catch up on the last few month's events. Keaton was the first to arrive, so Madison introduced him to her friends as her "business associate." A few sideways looks made her aware they knew she was fabricating the truth! The anticipation of the occasion continued.

Soft and easy listening music from the original 1972 soundtrack of the movie "Cabaret" was heard in the background. At the entrance to Madison's condo was a large vase of pink tulips mixed with red roses and finished with a champagne pink bow placed on a side table.

Once in the open-plan lounge and dining room, Madison offered her guests Kir Royale, literally a bubbly way to start the evening. It was a taste experience on its own, so she chose not to offer pre-dinner snacks.

Atmosphere

Stimulating conversation began immediately and continued from pre-dinner drinks right through to after dinner coffee, well after midnight. Everyone made an effort to integrate Keaton into their "circle." They found him easy to get along with and soon learned he had a broad range of conversation topics, was an active listener and had a keen sense of humor. They had no problems relaxing in his company and he was quick to win them over.

Madison was keen to spend as much time as she could with her guests. She had prepared all the food during the day and hired two students from a hotel school in the city to do the final finishing and help her with the serving. She asked them to wear black trousers, white shirt and a long black apron for their kitchen, serving duties and cleaning up duties. Her helpers were very attentive, had outgoing personalities and excellent serving skills.

In spite of the soft intimate glow produced by the many candles lit around the lounge and dining room, the atmosphere was full of chatter and laughter. The room also had dimmed side-lighting which provided warmth and accentuated Madison's latest artwork on the walls. She made liberal use of tulips and roses around the room, but they were not strongly scented. In the kitchen Madison had lit three chef's candles made from soy wax and designed to mask cooking odors from the seafood.

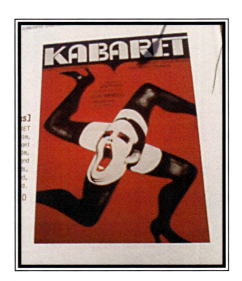

Generally Madison chose the more flirtatious yet reserved piano-based tunes common to light jazz and cabaret music. In a very subtle manner she chose to repeat three main tracks from Cabaret in her music playlist organized for the dinner party. These were "Maybe This Time", "Tomorrow Belongs To Me" and "Sitting Pretty." No-one seemed to pick up on this!

Appetite

At around 8:15pm, the serving staff lit the candles on the dining room table and filled the water glasses with iced mineral water. Madison led her guests to the dining room and everyone marveled at how elegant and stylish her table was. She gave it a classical uncluttered appearance that showed off her quality cutlery and array of Italian lead crystal glassware. The floral arrangements and candles remained in a line down the center of the table and were not required to be moved to make space available for serving platters. Madison had designed her menu to have all food pre-plated.

Madison placed her guests by alternating males and females around the table. Her serving staff placed the napkins on each person's lap, ladies first. She knew all their food preferences beforehand so was confident all tastes were catered for. They served the pre-plated appetizer and while the guests were eating were able to discreetly clear the champagne glasses from the lounge and take them to be washed.

Each time a new wine was offered, new glasses were used. Madison left the table to check all preparations in the kitchen before each course. The remainder of the time she had confidence in her earlier instructions and the server's skills to leave the presentation and service of the food to them.

Sufficient time between each course was given to allow a relaxed dining experience. Her friends enjoyed this time to start new conversation or reflect on the course they had just finished. Madison encouraged feedback and liked to receive constructive criticism.

Wine glasses were replenished when almost empty except if each guest indicated they had enoug. When servers were not required in the dining room they carefully and quietly went about cleaning up in the kitchen.

The menu Madison made was as follows:

Course	Menu item	Description	Matched with
Pre-dinner drinks	Champagne Kir Royale	Chilled champagne with creme de cassis	
Appetizer	Zucchini and pecorino salad	Thin ribbons of tender zucchini and shavings of pecorino drizzled with white truffle oil	No wine offered
Entrée	Oysters casino	Oysters grilled with bacon, minced shallots and garlic, chopped red pepper in a lemon parsley sauce	French Chablis
Sorbet	Champagne lime sorbet	Champagne sorbet made with zest and juice of fresh limes, garnished with a sprig of mint	
Main	Baked crayfish tails with a medley of spring vegetables	Baked crayfish tails with orange tarragon butter, served over asparagus, snow peas and cocktail tomatoes, sprinkled with roasted pinenuts and garnished with chopped spring onions, served on pates drizzled with balsamic vinegar.	Viognier or Pinot Gris for those who prefer white wine and a light Sirah for those who prefer red wine
Dessert	Strawberry and passion fruit sables	Sable cookies with a passion fruit and strawberry cream filling, garnishes with sliced strawberries and served on a mango couli	Muscat de Beaumes de Venise
Coffee	Freshly brewed espresso	Served with rosewater turkish delight	

Amusement

Madison did not organize any entertainment or activities during the entire dinner party. She was confident the food, conversation, music and ambiance would be sustainable throughout the night. She suggested coffee be served in the lounge for a change of scenery, but everyone was happy to stay at the table and carry on chatting.

Appreciation

No one left until close to one o'clock. They expressed their delight by thanking Madison and complimenting her on the evening.

Madison had individual red rose stems wrapped with cellophane and a ribbon for each guest. She gave it to them as they walked out the door as a token of their shared love of food, wine and good company. Her closest friend nudged her on the way out and whispered "Keaton, a business associate indeed?"

Madison thanked the two servers for making her hostess role so much easier. She was so happy with their work that she gave them a bonus and a free voucher to have a gourmet pizza at one of the popular pizzerias in town.

Everyone phoned at some stage during the week to say thank you for such a wonderful night. Keaton also phoned, but used the moment to suggest he prepared them a picnic-for-two in the country the next weekend.

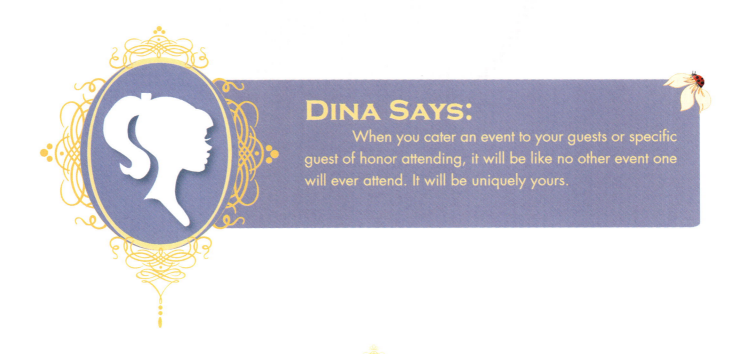

Dina Says:
When you cater an event to your guests or specific guest of honor attending, it will be like no other event one will ever attend. It will be uniquely yours.

Design and Plan Your Dinner Party

DIY party planners must be extremely well organized. Now that you have collected all your ideas, looked at as many magazines and talked with as many people as possible, it is time to get organized and start planning.

DIY dinner party components	Tasks handed over to a co-helper or party planner
Planning and design	Last minute food preparations
Manage own budget	Food service
Decorate the venue	Drink service
Write own invitations etc.	Clearing and cleaning
Plan own songs	
Coordinate the music	
Prepare own menu	
Organize own wine	
Do shopping for food and wine	
Polish cutlery and glassware	
Contact florist	
Do all food preparations	
Organize table setting	
Collect flowers	

Mood Board Ideas

Chapter 6: Final Project

Your A8 recipe planning sheet.

Visit the online Resource Library to download this worksheet.

Features	Notes, contact numbers, etc.
Attire	
Accessories	
Anticipation	
Arrival	
Atmosphere	
Appetite	
Amusement	
Appreciation	
DIY dinner party components	Tasks handed over to a co-helper or party planner

Mood Board Presentation

Decide on the best images that inspire you most about your planned dinner party. Position them on your mood board then share your design for others to give their feedback.

Good planning begins with a checklist. Visit the online Resource Library to download this worksheet:

<u>2-3 weeks before...</u>
- ☐ Set the budget
- ☐ Decide on the party style, time and location
- ☐ Decide guest list
- ☐ Decide on a theme
- ☐ Send out invitations
- ☐ Design menu and decide drink requirements
- ☐ Make or buy decorations and centerpieces
- ☐ Order food and drink supplies
- ☐ Organize party favors
- ☐ Decide on own dress
- ☐ Decide on accessories and purchase as necessary
- ☐ Check guest RSVPs and finalize guest list
- ☐ Hire extra refrigerators if necessary
- ☐ Plan music playlist

<u>A week before...</u>
- ☐ Pick up food and beverages
- ☐ Wrap the party favors

- ☐ Clean the house and surroundings
- ☐ Have the decorations ready to be put in place
- ☐ Place tables and chairs according to layout plan
- ☐ Have plenty of refrigeration and ice box space available
- ☐ Prepare food
- ☐ Chill wines and water

The day of the party...

- ☐ Meet with your helpers and check they know their responsibilities
- ☐ Collect flowers
- ☐ Set table
- ☐ Prepare food
- ☐ Make final checks of party space
- ☐ Refrigerate ready plated perishable food in covered serving dishes
- ☐ Plate non-perishable foods and leave covered on bench until service
- ☐ Get yourself dressed and ready to receive the first guests

Immediately after (within the next week)

- ☐ Clean up, wash up, pack up
- ☐ Receive compliments graciously
- ☐ Celebrate the success of the party

Glossary

A

Aioli – A garlic-flavored mayonnaise of Provence, served with fish and seafood and often with vegetables.

Amaretto – An Italian liqueur with a slightly bitter almond flavor.

Aperitif – A small wine or alcoholic liquor drink served as an appetizer or cocktail, taken to stimulate the appetite before a meal.

Armagnac – A dry, brown brandy distilled in the district of Armagnac, also known as Gers, in SW France.

Arugula – A Mediterranean plant of the mustard family, having pungent leaves used in salads.

Asti – A city in the Piedmont region of Italy, center of the wine producing region, and is famous for its sparkling wine.

Aubergine – European reference to eggplant.

B

Bavarois – Bavarian cream, which is a dessert made with custard, gelatin, and whipped cream.

Beef Wellington – A steak fillet covered with pate de foie gras, then wrapped in pastry and baked.

Bourguignon – A reduced red wine with onions, parsley, thyme, and butter.

Bulgur – A form of wheat that has been parboiled, cracked, and dried.

C

Cabaret – A restaurant or cafe that serves food and drink while offering music, a dance floor, and often entertainment of an improvisatory, satirical, and topical nature.

Cabernet Sauvignon – A premium dark red grape used in the making of a dry red wine, especially in the Bordeaux region of France and Northern California.

Calvados – A dry apple brandy distilled and made from apple cider in Normandy.

Canapes – A small, thin piece of bread or toast, spread with a savory topping like cheese, caviar, or anchovies.

Candelabra – A large ornamental branched holder for more than one candle.

Capsicum – A plant of the nightshade family, the common pepper of the garden, occurring in many varieties and used as a vegetable or ground as a condiment.

Carafes – An open-topped, wide-mouthed glass or metal container with a lip or spout, for holding and serving beverages, such as water or wine, at the table.

Carbonara – A sauce or dressing for spaghetti, usually containing minced prosciutto or pancetta, egg yolks, and grated cheese.

Cardamom – An aromatic seed capsule of a tropical Asian plant of the ginger family, used as a spice or condiment and also in medicine.

Carpaccio – An Italian appetizer of thinly sliced raw beef or fish served with a vinaigrette or other piquant sauce.

Cassoulet – A white haricot bean stew originating from France, often containing pork, mutton, garlic sausage, and preserved goose or duck.

Chardonnay – A white grape ordinarily grown in the Burgundy region of France, used in the making of a dry, white wine.

Chermoula – A marinade made from a mixture of herbs, oil, lemon juice, garlic, cumin, and salt, commonly used in Algerian, Moroccan and Tunisian cooking to flavor fish or seafood, but can also be used on other meats or vegetables.

Chicory – A blue-flower plant which is cultivated for its leaves in salads and its root roasted and ground as a coffee substitute.

Chutney – A sauce or relish of East Indian origin often compounded of both sweet and sour ingredients, such as fruits, herbs, sugar, spices, vinegar, and other seasonings.

Cointreau – A colorless, orange-flavored liqueur.

Compote – A dish of fruit stewed or cooked with sugar or in syrup, usually served as a dessert hot or cold.

Consommé – A clear soup made by boiling meat or chicken, bones, vegetables, etc., to extract their nutritive properties: served hot or jellied.

Coq au Vin – A French dish of chicken stewed in a sauce of red wine, diced pork, onions, garlic, and mushrooms.

Courgette – European reference to zucchini.

Couscous – A North American dish consisting of steamed semolina, served with vegetables and meat.

Crème Brulee – A custard that has been sprinkled with sugar and placed under a broiler until a brown crust forms on top.

Crème de Cassis – A liqueur flavored cream with black currants.

Cruet – A small glass bottle or container, especially one for holding salt, pepper, vinegar, oil, etc., for the table.

#

Decorum – An observance or requirement of proper behavior, speech, dress, etc., typically of polite society.

Demi-glace – A rich brown sauce in French cuisine used by itself or as a base for other sauces.

Demi-tasse – A small cup for serving strong black coffee after dinner or a meal.

Dietary – Of or pertaining to a diet, a regulated allowance of food.

Digestif – A drink of brandy, liqueur, etc., taken after a meal to aid the digestion.

Dignitary – A person who holds a high rank or office, as in the government or church.

F

Feta – A soft, white, brine-cured Greek cheese made from sheep or goat milk.

Fillet Mignon – A small, tender round of steak cut from the thick end of a beef tenderloin.

French Chablis – A Chardonnay or dry white wine renown for the purity of its aroma and taste, produced in the town of Chablis.

Frittata – An Italian omelet dish made with eggs resembling a large pancake and containing chopped vegetables or meat, seasonings, and often ricotta, Parmesan, or other cheese.

G

Gateau – A richly decorated cake, especially a very light sponge cake with a rich icing or filling.

Gazpacho – A soup made of chopped tomatoes, cucumbers, onions, garlic, oil, and vinegar, and served cold.

Gewürztraminer – A type of white grape used in making a dry white table wine in Germany, the Alsace region of France, and Northern California.

Gnocchi – A dish of little dumplings made from potatoes, semolina pasta, flour, or a combination of these ingredients, used to garnish soup or served alone with sauce.

Goblet – A bowl-shaped drinking glass with a foot and stem.

Grand Marnier – A brand of French liqueur having a brandy base and an orange flavor.

J

Jus – French reference to sauce, gravy or juice.

K

Kameez – A long tunic worn by many people from the Indian subcontinent, usually along with a shalwar.

Kir Royale – An aperitif of dry white wine or sometimes champagne, flavored with cassis.

L

Langoustine – A large prawn or small lobster used for food.

Leek – A plant of the amaryllis family, allied to the onion, having a cylindrical white bulb, stem, and leaves used in cooking.

Lobster Newburg – Lobster cooked in a thick, rich seasoned cream sauce made with sherry or brandy.

Lyonnaise – A food, such as fried potatoes, that is cooked or garnished with pieces of onion.

M

Macerated – To have softened or separated and broken up into parts by steeping, or soaking, in a liquid.

Madeira – A rich, strong, and fortified white or amber wine, resembling sherry, receiving its name from where it is made.

Mascarpone – A very soft Italian cream cheese made from cow's milk.

Muscat de Beaumes de Venise – A sweet fortified wine of the many appellations produced in the eastern central region of the southern half of the Rhone Valley.

N

Nonic – A variation of the iconic, traditional beer glass that is slender, but shorter and stouter with a mouth that bulges out from the top to help partially improve grip and prevent the glasses from sticking together when stacked.

Nougatine – A chocolate-coated nougat.

O

Orzo – A pasta in the form of small rice-like grains, shaped like pearls of barley, and frequently prepared with lamb in Greek cuisine.

Osso Bucco – A stew, originally from Italy, made with knuckle of veal, cooked in tomato sauce.

P

Panforte – A traditional Italian dessert containing fruits and nuts, resembling fruitcake.

Panna Cotta – A cold, light, molded egg, custard flavored with crème caramel.

Pate – a paste or spread made of pureed or finely chopped liver, meat, fish, game, etc., served as a hors d'oeuvres

Pavlova – A meringue cake topped with whipped cream and fruit.

Pecorino – A dry, hard, pungent Italian cheese made from ewe's milk, especially Romano.

Pesto – A sauce typically made with basil leaves, pine nuts, garlic, olive oil, and grated Parmesan blended together and served hot or cold over pasta, fish, or meat.

Petits Fours – A small teacake, variously frosted and decorated.

Pilsner – A tall glass that is tapered to a short stem at the bottom, used especially for a pale, light lager beer.

Pinot – Any of several varieties of purple or white vinifera grapes yielding a red or white wine, used especially in making burgundies and champagnes.

Pinot Blanc – A white wine made from white vinifera grapes, with possible hints of pear flavors and aromas.

Pinot Gris – A white Italian wine made from white grapes, with possible hints of green apple flavors and aromas.

Pinot Noir – A red wine made from purple vinifera grapes.

Ponzu – A citrus-based sauce made from orange juice, sake, sugar, soy sauce, and red pepper, commonly used in Japanese cuisine and is very tart in flavor, with a thin, watery consistency and a light yellow color.

Prosciutto – A salted Italian ham that has been cured by drying, always sliced paper-thin for serving, usually as a hors d'oeuvre.

Q

Quiche – A savory pie-like tart dish consisting of an unsweetened pastry shell filled with rich custard and usually containing cheese and other ingredients, such as vegetables, seafood, bacon, or ham.

R

Ricotta – A soft, white, unsalted Italian cheese made from sheep's milk that resembles cottage cheese, used especially in making ravioli and gnocchi.

Riesling – A variety of grape, the vine bearing this grape is usually grown in Europe and California, and is used to create a fragrant, white, dry or sweet wine.

Rocket leaves – An edible plant, commonly known as arugula, that has a rich, peppery taste and its leaves are frequently used in salads.

S

Saffron – A crocus having purple and white flowers with orange stigmas, commonly called "vegetable gold" due to the color and it being the world's most expensive spice, its stigmas are dried and processed into an orange-colored condiment to be used for coloring and flavoring foods.

Saris – A traditional dress garment worn by Hindu women of India, Pakistan, etc., consisting of a long and narrow piece of cotton or silk cloth elaborately swathed or wrapped around the body with one end draped over the head or over one shoulder.

Sauvignon – A small blue-black grape grown primarily in the Medoc region of Bordeaux, in SW France, and highly prized in winemaking.

Sauvignon Blanc – A white grape grown primarily in France and California, commonly made into a table wine.

Schnitzel – A cutlet, especially of veal.

Serviette – A small square of cloth or paper used as a table napkin while eating to protect clothes or wipe the mouth and hands with.

Shallots – A plant related to the onion, having a divided bulb which separates into small sections and is used for flavoring in cookery.

Shalwar – A pair of loose-fitting, pajama-like trousers worn by both men and women in India and Southeast Asia, tapering to a narrow fit around the ankles.

Shiraz (Syrah) – A red grape grown in France and Australia, used often in a blend for making wine.

Siennese – Of or pertaining to Sienna, a city of Italy.

Souffle – A light baked dish made fluffy with beaten egg whites combined with egg yolks, white sauce, and fish, cheese, or other ingredients.

Stilton – a rich, waxy, white cheese, veined with mold: made principally in England.

T

Tabbouleh – A salad of fine-ground bulgur, parsley, tomatoes, green onions, mint, olive oil, and lemon juice.

Tagliatelle – A form of egg noodle pasta cut into long, narrow, flat strip pieces.

Tannic – A wine having an astringent taste imparted by the presence of tannic acid.

Tapas – A snack or appetizer, typically served with wine or beer.

Tarragon – An aromatic perennial plant having whitish flowers and small toothed leaves, which are used as a seasoning.

Tartin – A fancy French open-faced sandwich, especially one with a rich or elaborate topping, such as a jam or butter.

Tenderloin – A tender cut of beef muscle lying between the sirloin and ribs.

Terrine – A pate or similar casserole-like dish of chopped meat, game, fish, or vegetables baked in such a dish and served cold.

Tiramisu – An Italian dessert with coffee and liquor-soaked layers of sponge cake alternating with mascarpone cheese and chocolate.

Torte – A rich cake originating in Austria, especially one containing little or no flour, usually made with eggs and ground nuts or bread crumbs and decorated or filled with cream, fruit, nuts, and jam.

Turmeric – A powder prepared from an Asian plant of the ginger family, used as a condiment, as in curry powder, or as a yellow dye.

U

Udon – A thick, white Japanese noodle made from wheat flour, and often served in soup.

V

Vichyssoise – A cream soup of potatoes and leeks, usually served chilled and often garnished with chopped chives.

Viognier – A white wine grape, the only one permitted for the French wine Condrieu, which is turned into a wine and is sometimes blended with Chardonnay.

Vitrified (Vitreous) – To convert or be converted into glass or a glassy substance.

Lovegevity's Wedding Planning Institute

© 2014 - Copyright by Lovegevity, Inc. All Rights Reserved.